To: Ra "
Be
read my story *fan*

4-10-13 *Rosie Weary*
1 Cor. 15:58

Stepping Out From the Shadows

by Rosie Camper Weary
with Alexis Spencer-Byers

R.E.A.L. Publishing
Richland, Mississippi

Stepping Out From the Shadows

Copyright © 2010 Rosie Camper Weary

All rights reserved. No part of this book, contents or cover may be reproduced, or transmitted in any form or by any means, electronic or mechanical, including photocopying, recording, or by any information storage or retrieval system without permission in writing from the publisher.

Library of Congress Cataloging-in-Publication data is on file

ISBN-13 978-0-9832105-0-4
ISBN-10 0-9832105-0-0

Printed and bound in the United States of America
First printing

All Scripture quotations, unless otherwise indicated, are taken from the *New King James Version*. Copyright © 1979, 1980, 1982 by Thomas Nelson, Inc. Used by permission. All rights reserved.

For information, please contact: **R.E.A.L. Publishing**
1 (601) 932-1101 or realpublishing@gmail.com

Endorsements

Most people who have had the opportunity to work with Rosie (whom I know and cherish both as my sister-in-law and as a long-time co-laborer for the Kingdom) can attest to her quietness. She is ever willing to take on all tasks and learns quickly to do well those that she has no previous experience with. This book is indicative that her quietness masked her inner voices of dignity, questioning, fears and rage over the injustices that she experienced and witnessed. This book is a truly worthwhile effort in describing her personal journey towards completeness. It helps the reader to understand that following God's calling is not the joy-filled perfect life; rather, it is the perfected life that comes when Jesus is the center of your life. Thank you, Rosie, for teaching us about bearing up in victories, giving up pain, and finding joy in the new day.

Cornelius J. Jones
Board Chairman, South Central Community Action Agency

I am so thankful to have been Rosie Weary's friend and fellow believer in Christ for almost 30 years. Rosie's commitment to ministry and example of leadership continues to inspire. Her story is illuminating, and anyone who reads this book will be grateful that Rosie decided to "step out from the shadows." She is vulnerable and real, and she shares experiences that most of us who are serious about following the Lord can identify with, including the joys, sorrows, doubts and certainties. Her openness gives all of us permission to ask the Lord why, when there seem to be no answers to our deepest questions. This book is a must-read, and I happily recommend it.

Kathy Dudley
Partner, Dudley & Associates
Founder and former President, Voice of Hope Ministries

Rosie Weary says, "Listening is something I've always been good at." This is why her book is so valuable to read and listen to: because she tells her story with an honest, warm integrity that reflects a life of someone who has carefully listened to God, to others and to herself through both joy and sorrow. This is not just an inspirational story of a poor girl raised in rural Mississippi who becomes the wife of a nationally known Christian leader. It is also an educational story about race and family that oozes wisdom and a great faith in a faithful God. Enjoy listening to her!

Robert Fryling
Publisher, InterVarsity Press

It is said that, there is nothing more powerful than a good story. We love to hear them because they speak to us at a gut level. Stories don't speak to us on just one sensory level but engage all five senses at once, causing us to have a virtual experience with the storyteller. Rosie is a very good storyteller, her words are full of life and she expresses herself well. You can tell she is still in touch with the smells ,the sounds, and the feelings of the events as she shares them with us. Good stories cause us to see life through the storytellers eyes. Rosie has caused us to see life through her eyes. Life is not always pretty but it is powerful. Thank you Rosie, because your book has made me, as the youth say, 'feel you' !

Bishop Ronnie Crudup
New Horizon Church International, Jackson, MS

God led and accompanied Rosie Weary through her childhood, her desire to leave Mississippi, and her return to Mississippi; through the struggle for civil rights for black people in rural Mississippi; through the pangs and changes of a growing outreach ministry; and through the joys, trials and tragedies of being a wife and mother. This is a story well worth reading, because we learn from Rosie that God will lead and accompany each of us who desire to follow Him, no matter the circumstances.

John Rhine
Volunteer, The Mendenhall Ministries

This book is dedicated to those whom I love and care about:

My husband of 40 years, Dolphus Weary, who has always pushed me to step out of the shadows and be all that God created me to be;

My children, Danita and Ryan, and grandson, Li'l Reggie— and our special son, Reggie, who was killed in a tragic car accident in 2004; and

My siblings, who have always been there for me.

Proceeds from the sell of this book are used to fund a rural Christian foundation that will help build Christian leaders and ministries for years to come.

Contents

Acknowledgments

Even though I was initially reluctant to write this book, I am grateful to all who pushed me and encouraged me to share my story. I want to acknowledge and thank a few of those individuals.

Dolphus Weary, who has encouraged me for years to write this book.

The Board of REAL Christian Foundation, who have stood with me and allowed me the freedom to write it.

My staff: Linda Jackson, Virginia Chase and Crystal Cline, who have picked up the slack in the office so that I could have the time to concentrate on this project.

My sisters Vera and Earlene, and my brother Ernest, Jr., who helped with details about our family and our childhood that were foggy in my mind.

My dear friend Virginia Walker, who constantly reminds me of my value as a child of God and how He wants me to be transparent and real.

Our church family, whose love and prayers are priceless. The teachings I've received there have helped to guide me in life and ministry.

For all of those who contributed funds in order that I might get this book published.

For Alexis Spencer-Byers for the countless hours spent in helping to shape my story into a publishable manuscript.

I'd be remiss if I did not give my God the ultimate thanks. Without Him, there would be no story to tell.

Foreword

Folks reading Rosie's story weren't around in 1857, 1863, 1865, 1868, 1870, or 1896. Decisions made in those years changed history.

Some of us were around in 1954. I was in the sixth grade. In very segregated Washington, DC. Brown v. Board of Education. This decision had a profound effect on my life. No, it was not a decision that permitted me to go to a "White School" for the first time. As a Caucasian child, I had been permitted to go to those schools from the day I started first grade. But all those years I had been bothered by something not just related to school. I could never understand why there were drinking fountains with signs over them that said, "Colored." Why did some public restrooms say, "White Only"? I questioned why "Colored" people had to go to the back of the bus. As an 11-year-old child, I had become uncomfortable with the way things were. That Supreme Court decision came at a time in my life when I could comprehend and act. "Blacks" became an important part of my life.

In the early '60s, as a student at Florida State University, I had the privilege of escorting and mentoring the first African-American student at FSU—Max Courtney. Max graduated in 1965, as did I. A few years later, I was married and in Washington, DC. Max had also moved to DC. Max and I could meet for lunch during the week, and I have fond memories of Max entertaining my husband and me in his apartment. Defining dates and events of my life are relevant to my friendship with the Wearys.

Probably many of Rosie's readers were around in 1950, 1968 and 1970. Those were key dates for Rosie. Sure, Rosie's life has been filled with other dates of significance; but, for a few minutes think about what happened in those three years. Rosie was born; she left Mississippi to go to Los Angeles for college; she married Dolphus. Where were you living, and what were you experiencing in those years? In terms of segregation or integration? In terms of who your friends were; where you lived, shopped, and went to the movies? If you lived somewhere other than the Deep South, were you aware of what was really going on in that area of our country? Thinking about your life in those years provides an important backdrop for reading Rosie's story. Were you aware of the increasingly significant events of 1955, 1960, 1962, 1963, 1964, 1965 and 1968? Sure, all readers have undoubtedly heard Martin Luther King Jr.'s 1963 "I Have a Dream" speech and seen pictures of the hundreds of thousands of participants in the "March on Washington." You get inspired by that speech, and then, just five years later, you are grieved and angered by Dr. King's assassination in Memphis.

Fast forward to the final decade of the 20th century. Among the standouts of the 1990s for me—I met Dolphus Weary. We were on the board of ECFA (Evangelical Council for Financial Accountability) together. As our friendship developed, I heard about Rosie and their three kids. Our friendship grew when we later served together on the World Vision board, and I finally got to meet Rosie! The woman I had heard so much about and I became friends. This brings us to today and what awaits you in the following pages: a story of hope, despair, gumption, faith, romance, work, friends, prayer, family and triumph.

I'm thankful for my friendship with Dolphus and Rosie. Having read and given Dolphus's book to friends, I was so pleased that Rosie had finally been convinced to tell her story. It's a compelling one. You will be challenged to put yourself in Rosie's place and consider what you would have done as you developed from a child of poverty in Mississippi, to someone stepping out and going to LA for college with essentially no money and not even surety of admission, to a young woman marrying someone who wanted to return to the place from which they had both "escaped," to a young mother, to a person who came to understand that Jesus wanted a personal relationship with her, to a woman who needed to find her niche, to a mother who had to go through the tragedy of the loss of a child, to a person now heading a foundation that provides opportunities for people in rural Mississippi who had childhoods like those of Rosie and Dolphus.

If you haven't had the pleasure of meeting Rosie in person, you will meet her through her story...

Joyce Godwin
Albuquerque, New Mexico
June 2010

Introduction: Coming Full Circle

It was a long way to go to get back to where I'd begun.

Fifty-plus years earlier and an ocean away, my siblings and I (all ten of us) had spent many a hot summer afternoon circled in our yard, playing games. "A tisket, a tasket," we'd chant, "I lost my yellow basket." Eventually, whoever was "it" would shake his or her hip at one of the others, and a new round would begin.

Poor, black and young in Mississippi as the Civil Rights Movement gained steam, we were at first largely oblivious to the reshaping of our nation that was already underway. Later, of course, we would become aware of the racial injustices all around us and would, in a variety of ways, seek to make things better for ourselves, our neighbors, and our children. But back then our window on the world was small, and our days were filled with simple things: playing games together, carrying water so Mama could tend her flowers, throwing a baseball with Daddy (whom many said could have played professionally, if they had allowed Blacks in the league back then), going fishing, and helping on our family farm.

Now, on my first-ever visit to Africa, I watch the children of Liberia play games remarkably similar to those my brothers and sisters and I played. I observe the extreme poverty in which they live, I feel the oppressive heat of the midday sun, and I am transported back to my own childhood.

Often, a circle serves as a symbol of futility. Except in childhood games and at racetracks, "going around in circles" is not considered to be a good thing. The feeling that we've gone and gone, but gotten nowhere, frustrates us terribly. There is an element of that for me on this visit to the Motherland. How is it that people still live like this? In 2009? Hasn't the world made more progress than this?

On the other hand, circles remind us of our connectedness—to one another, to our own pasts, and to the lessons we've learned from the experiences and people who have come before. I was a history major in college because learning about where we came from has always fascinated me.

So as we drive past the mud huts and rickety tin-roofed shacks, with no electricity or running water, I feel sadness, but I am also filled with hope. Because the Mississippi of my childhood—the Mississippi this place reminds me so much of—is not the Mississippi I live in today. Because my life has changed, and I have changed, and I can be connected without being trapped. And because my husband, Dolphus, and I—both raised in the deep shadows of poverty and racism—have been invited to this country as honored guests. Dolphus has addressed churches, colleges and business and military leaders, while I have spoken to the children. We have met with government officials.

And in so doing, we have learned not only about Liberia's recent past—the devastating tribal war they endured for fifteen years—but also about the plans for this nation's future. We hear how many have returned to the Lord, how the newly elected President is a Christian, and how there is a desire to rebuild the country on the basis of Christian principles. A Liberian woman testifies that while things are still much worse than they were before the war, they are much better than they were a year ago. We experience the kindness and generosity of people here—a generosity that wells up out of poverty, as the Apostle Paul exhorts—and we feel certain that the relationships we've forged during these eleven days will last. There is a sense of connectedness to this place and these people.

As I look back over my life—my journey thus far—I realize how filled it is with circles. From those early games, symbolic of the strong family ties I've been privileged to experience, to the grant-making foundation Dolphus and I began a dozen years ago to assist small rural ministries like the one we had just left after more than 25 years of service, I find myself, over and over again, reaching back, reaching out, maintaining connection with those around me in the hope that we can all move forward together.

I have never been an out-front kind of person. I don't enjoy the spotlight, and public speaking absolutely terrifies me. So when my husband and the Board of our foundation encouraged me to write a book—to tell my story—I resisted. What could I possibly have to say that people would want to read? Why would they be interested in my life—a life that feels so ordinary so much of the time? When I think about how to describe myself, what comes to mind are words like: simple, humble, timid, not aggressive, sometimes selfish, envious of others' gifts and abilities, caring, compassionate, learning to be grateful... Some good things, some bad things, some things that are neither positive nor negative, but nothing that strikes me as being particularly interesting or book-worthy.

No, book-writing has always seemed like something other people should do. People like Dolphus: people who have risen from impoverished beginnings to positions of leadership and influence, and who love to tell the story of how that transformation happened. Who can address any audience—members of small country churches, a developing African military, international Boards of Directors, White House Bible study participants, and worshippers at the National Cathedral—and have their listeners hanging on their every word. Not people like me, who shake and sweat when asked to address a group of children; who have spent their whole professional lives working in a series of secretarial, administrative and other support roles; whose greatest claim to fame is being married to somebody a lot of people have heard of...

Thoughts like these remind me of something else my life has been filled with—shadows. Some are easily identifiable: the poverty and racism I mentioned before, the tragic loss of a child, struggles with depression and poor self-image. Others are trickier: things that aren't bad but still have the potential to hide me from the sun, like being a quiet woman who is married to a ministry leader with a forceful personality.

And I've realized that these are the stories I need to tell. Because maybe what I've learned about living in shadows—and about finding ways to emerge from them—can be helpful to someone else. Maybe my little story can help others to trust God, to find joy and fulfillment in behind-the-scenes acts of service, to figure out how to stand up for themselves without being disrespectful, and to put one foot in front of the other, over and over again, even if it sometimes feels like they're going in circles.

My main concern, as I prepare to share my story with anyone who wants to hear it, is that people may think I'm blaming others (my husband among them) for my failures, especially for my inability to speak up for myself early in our marriage and ministry. Others might think when I talk about my growth in this area, that I'm encouraging spouses to rebel against each other. I'm not trying to do either of these things. I take full responsibility for the poor self-image and lack of courage that kept me from being a full participant in decisions about my own life and work for many years. My deep-seated fears were what made it hard for me to reach my full God-given potential and kept me from being the best ambassador for Christ that I could be.

I praise God that He has done so much to free me from those doubts and fears! (It's a journey, and I still have a ways to go, but He has brought me so far.) I praise Him also for my wonderful husband, who has encouraged me to grow into the person God wants me to be. I can honestly say that as I have become more self-confident and even assertive, our marriage has grown stronger, and we are better able to function as a unified team. And I praise Him for allowing me to spend these last 39 years in ministry. Despite my flaws and struggles, I do believe that God has used me to bless others, and I am profoundly grateful for that.

So I pray that people will read and receive my story as I intend it: as a reflection on my own struggles and growth, and as a testimony to the liberating power of God working in my life.

As I think about the part of my life that now lies behind me, I remember the words of a Chinese philosopher named Lao Tzu: "A journey of a thousand miles begins with a single step." This has certainly been my experience. Life, change, growth—these things don't generally happen in thousand-mile leaps. They happen in very ordinary-sized steps.

Some steps are relatively easy to take. Sometimes we have a clear sense of direction, the road ahead is flat and well-paved, the scenery is pleasant, and we've even managed to equip ourselves with shoes appropriate to the terrain. Other steps are much more daunting.

In Mississippi, especially in low-lying areas with poor drainage, we have a lot of flash-flooding. Whenever there's a heavy rain, we're reminded not to drive into any pool of water we can't see the bottom of, because there's no way to know what may have happened to the road beneath. Literally speaking, this is sound advice. Figuratively, though, we're sometimes called to venture into such pools. Our only reason to expect that solid ground lies ahead is Jesus' promise never to leave or forsake us. We have to believe that God will bring us through—and we have to understand that His faithfulness doesn't guarantee that we will come through unscathed, only that we will come through, and that He will be beside us as we do.

Although I didn't realize it at the time, God was preparing me from the very beginning of my life to take steps of faith…

Chapter One
Stepping Out In Faith: Black and broke at a white Christian college

From before I was born until I was about four or five, my family lived "across the creek." The only thing that connected our house and farm to the road that led to the nearby town of Pinola, Mississippi, was a "bridge" made out of a single large fallen tree. My older brothers and sisters walked across that tree to go to school, and many Sundays (if the mule wagon wasn't available), we all walked across it to get to church.

I distinctly remember the first time I crossed the creek as a young child. With my brothers holding my hands, we inched across the tree trunk, single-file. It was high above the water, and I didn't know how to swim, so I was completely terrified. Adding to my fear was the fact that my brothers had told me all sorts of stories about the "stinging snakes" and water moccasins that lived in the creek below.

When it rained, the water would cover that tree, and we'd have to walk along the creek to a different one that was even higher up (and, of course, slippery in the wet weather). I was so scared to step onto this second tree that one of my brothers would carry me across on his back whenever we had to use it.

The prospect of crossing the creek filled me with dread every time, and yet, amazingly, not one of us ever fell into the water, cracked our heads on a rock, got bitten by a snake, or came to any other kind of harm while walking this natural high-wire. Looking back, I see the hand of God protecting us as we took those dangerous steps on unsteady ground.

Many years later, I would take a different kind of faith step when I went off to college. Like in those early days crossing the creek, I had to trust both God and people He brought into my life for protection and provision.

I had flourished in high school, graduating second in my class (out of 61 seniors) at Pinola's New Hymn High School in May of 1968. Kids from New Hymn who went to college almost always attended one of the state's three black public universities: Alcorn State, Jackson State or Mississippi Valley State. Occasionally, someone might go to Tougaloo College, Piney Woods Junior College, or Prentiss Institute (also a junior college), but since these are private schools, they are much more expensive and therefore were out of reach for most families in my home community. Despite James Meredith's enrollment at the University of Mississippi a few years earlier, it was still extremely difficult and unpopular for a black student to attend any of Mississippi's five white public universities.

During my senior year, New Hymn's principal, Mr. Gray, called me into his office. He told me that Alcorn was offering academic scholarships to the students graduating highest in their classes, and he helped me complete an application. When Alcorn accepted me and offered a full scholarship, I naturally assumed that I would go there—what other good option could there possibly be?

But that summer, I attended a Sunday School Institute in Mendenhall, Mississippi, as a delegate from my church, New Zion Baptist in Pinola. The Institute was hosted by Voice of Calvary Ministries (VOC), which had been founded by John and Vera Mae Perkins a few years earlier. Rev. and Mrs. Perkins had both grown up in rural Mississippi. As young adults, they moved to California, but then God called them back to their home state. They returned in 1960 and immediately began leading Bible studies in several schools in the area (including New Hymn). They would go into any school or college that would have them, teaching the Word of God to young people. They also spearheaded civil rights activities in the local community, and their ministry was growing rapidly.

One of the VOC staff members was a young man named Dolphus Weary. Dolphus, after spending two years at Piney Woods Junior College, had decided to complete his undergraduate education at Los Angeles Baptist College (LABC), on a basketball scholarship. He had already spent one year at LABC by this time, and he would be returning for one more. My best friend, Carolyn Albritton (who graduated first in our class), was on staff with VOC that summer, as well. Carolyn had been accepted at LABC and would be starting there in the fall.

Carolyn, Dolphus and I spent a lot of time together that summer, at the Institute and other VOC activities, and later at Cedine Bible Camp in Tennessee. The topic of LABC came up frequently.

"Why don't you come, too?" Carolyn would suggest. "It'll be great!"

Dolphus encouraged me to consider applying as well. "This would be a really good opportunity for you, Rosie. You'll get to study the Bible, but you can also major in other subjects."

This was the right selling point for me because while I did yearn to study the Bible and learn more about Jesus, I also wanted to use my college education to prepare for a teaching career. Teachers were pretty much the only professional role models we had in the local black community at that time (I'd read about black doctors in the North, but I didn't know of any in Mississippi), so I had decided I should be one.

Los Angeles Baptist College had something else going for it as well: It was in Los Angeles. My teaching aspirations were based primarily on pragmatism. My real dream was to become a fashion model, and California seemed like it would be the perfect place to pursue a career in modeling.

More generally speaking, California promised an escape from the crushing poverty I had known my whole life. Other people from our community had gone off to California and other far-away states, and from time to time they would come back to Mississippi to attend a family reunion or church revival, wearing fancy clothes and driving expensive cars. (Later I would learn that some of those cars were rented, and oftentimes people had gone into debt to attain the appearance of prosperity, but at the time I didn't know any of that.) I was determined not to be poor any more, and going to California definitely seemed like a step in the right direction.

Rev. Perkins also began encouraging me to think about applying to LABC. The more he, Dolphus and Carolyn talked about it and nudged me in that direction, the more appealing the idea became. About halfway through the summer, I told Rev. Perkins that I had decided I wanted to apply. He helped me write a letter to the school, and I sent it off. They responded and encouraged me to submit an official application. So I did, but I didn't hear anything else before it was time for Dolphus, Carolyn and two other young people from the area to leave for Los Angeles. I had to choose between the safe, secure, well-provisioned path laid out for me in Mississippi and the unfamiliar, precarious road that led to California with no guarantees about what awaited me at the other end.

Dolphus and Carolyn tried to reassure me. "They need more minority students," Dolphus explained. "I'm certain they'll accept you, and you can get work study and a grant to help pay the tuition."

"Let's just trust you're going to be accepted," Carolyn exhorted me.

With my friends at Voice of Calvary all encouraging me, I decided that I would go, believing not only that I would be accepted by the college, but also that I would receive enough financial aid to pay for my education.

Because without financial aid, there was no way I could afford to go to any college. I had worked a little bit for my father during the summer, picking cucumbers, but because I had spent so much time participating in VOC activities, I didn't make nearly as much money as I had planned. My total income for the summer ended up being $19, and some of that had to go toward school supplies and clothes.

My parents had been less enthusiastic than my friends about my choice of college, for a number of reasons, money being only one of them. "Why are you going so far away?" they asked. "Why not stay closer to home?" I'm sure they were petrified about sending their daughter off into the unknown. But when they realized how much I wanted to go, and saw that my mind was made up anyway, they stopped trying to convince me to stay in Mississippi.

My mother even told my father to give me some money for college. He gave me $40, which was a lot for them but wouldn't go far toward paying my $5,000 tuition bill.

As the time drew near for us to leave, and I still hadn't heard from LABC, my faith did waver a little bit. Mississippi colleges start earlier than California schools, and I had made no arrangements with Alcorn, so that door was closing quickly.

"What am I going to do?" I asked myself. "I want to go to school somewhere. I don't want to lose my scholarship and have nowhere to go. What if I've messed this up?"

Adding to my doubts, I knew that some of my cousins had been skeptical of my decision. "Rosie thinks she's all that, going out there. But she'll be back." Though their words echoed my own fears, they also fueled my determination to make it. I would show them that I could do this. I shook off my anxiety as best I could and prepared for the journey.

The day came for us to leave, and five of us crammed into a Volkswagen bug to make the long drive. Dolphus and his friend and basketball teammate, Jimmie Walker, sat in the front seats. Carolyn and I shared the back seat with a woman named Rachel Brown. Rachel was a few years older, but also a freshman, having spent some time living in St. Louis after high school. Rev. and Mrs. Perkins came to pray for us before we left. After the prayer time, Rev. Perkins asked me a question.

"I know you didn't get to work much this summer, Rosie. How much money have you got?"

I had bought an overcoat, a trunk, sheets and a few other necessities out of my summer earnings and my father's gift. "I have $9," I told Rev. Perkins. He looked concerned but didn't say anything else, and we pulled away, stuffed like sardines into a car with no air conditioning, with 2,000 miles of road ahead of us.

We were in that car so long I didn't think we'd ever get to California. These were the dog days of summer, and the heat was nearly unbearable. We got to Blythe, California, at three or four in the morning, and it was still so hot we could barely breathe. We didn't stop to see any of the sights along the way (we just watched the signs go by as we drove past), and we didn't spend the night anywhere, we just drove. At least, Dolphus and Jimmie drove; we girls simply sat, shoulder to shoulder, in the back seat.

Our only stops were for gas—so if you didn't use the bathroom then, you'd be in trouble. At one of the gas stations, a sign posted on the door reminded us that escaping racial discrimination was not going to be quick or easy. "Outhouses for coloreds," the sign informed us. We didn't want any trouble (we had our sights set on a goal, and we couldn't afford to be slowed down), so we used the outhouses and kept going.

Nearly 20 years later, in the 1980s, Dolphus and I would drive to California again. At a stop in Texas, I asked the woman working at the gas station register where the restrooms were. She pointed outside. Then I noticed an indoor restroom and a white woman heading toward it. Again, I decided the risk of trouble was too great. Again, I used an outhouse located only a few yards from working indoor facilities.

When we finally arrived at LABC, and I got my first glimpse of the campus, it took my breath away. The surrounding area was dry and brown, but the well-watered college grounds were lush and green, covered with trees, beautiful flowers and ice plants. (I had never seen an ice plant before, and I had no idea what it was, but it was lovely.) At the top of a hill sat the two-story dormitory—a gorgeous stone building with a pool in front. Down the hill and across the highway were classroom buildings and a new gymnasium (the gym had been completed the year Dolphus and Jimmie enrolled). Administrative offices, the cafeteria, the library and the President's house also dotted the landscape. I was a world away from the cotton fields, dirt roads and rickety shacks of Mississippi, and it was a dream come true—assuming, of course, that I would be allowed to stay.

One thing I noticed immediately was that there were very few people on campus. We soon found out why: All the students were away at a pre-semester retreat. A young woman had been sent to pick Carolyn, Rachel and me up and bring us to the girls' retreat, so that seemed like a good sign. At least they were expecting me!

We were sweaty from the drive, and still wearing the same clothes we'd had on when we left Mississippi, but there was no time to change. At the retreat, I met my roommate: a young white woman who was an upperclassman and engaged to be married. Carolyn, Rachel and I were the only black women (out of about 100) there. We had missed the first part of the retreat, but we arrived in time for a presentation about what would be expected of us as LABC students.

The whole experience was uncomfortable and unsettling, and I spent a good part of the time asking myself, "What in the world are you doing here?" I felt lost among all these young white women who seemed to belong there. A few of them spoke to us, and I appreciated that, but I still felt awkward, isolated and out of place.

Once the retreat was over, I went to the registrar's office, where they confirmed that I had in fact been accepted to the college. That was the good news. The bad news was that while I qualified for a loan and work-study, my application had been submitted too late for me to get a grant. The grant would have covered a large portion of my tuition, so not having it was going to be a significant hurdle to overcome.

Around that time, a letter arrived in the mail for me. It was from John and Vera Mae Perkins. Inside the envelope, there was also a check for $25.

The generosity of people who have little themselves is humbling and overwhelming. I deposited that check into a bank account Dolphus had opened in California, and it was a long time before I touched any of that money.

In the meantime, I thought maybe I could work enough to cover my tuition and other expenses. I got a work-study job in the school cafeteria, and I also applied for a part-time position at a local hospital. During the interview, I was asked if I had ever worked with blood. I said no.

The interviewer asked, "Do you think you can?"

I couldn't come up with any answer but the truth: "I don't know."

I didn't get the job.

Starting to get desperate, I wrote a letter to my mother, and she sent me $30—$15 for me, and $15 for the school. That would be the last of the money I'd get from my family for college. My parents, neither of whom had finished high school, were determined that all of their children should graduate, and, to their credit, we all did. But while they were supportive of my desire to go to college, that hadn't ever really been something they pushed—I think it was just too far outside their own experience and expectations—and it certainly wasn't something they were able to finance.

Soon I started getting notices in my campus mailbox: I would be sent home if I didn't take care of my bill. I was working as much as I could, friends and family had given me what they could, and it still wasn't enough. I had no idea how that bill was going to get paid. I remembered my cousins predicting that I'd soon be back in Mississippi, and I lived in fear that they would turn out to be right.

One day, Dolphus got a note in his mailbox. Several of the black students were being summoned to the President's office for a meeting. Carolyn was not on the list, but I was.

We talked anxiously amongst ourselves as we awaited that Sunday afternoon appointment. "What's happening?" we asked each other. "Do you think they're going to send us home?" We feared the worst, but it turned out to be something completely different.

We walked into the President's outer office, where Ms. Harriet Ishii normally sat. Ms. Ishii was an Asian woman, and she was always very kind to students—which was comforting when you found yourself in the President's office. But this was Sunday, so Ms. Ishii wasn't there, and we were on our own in that imposing space. Soon Dr. Duncan emerged from his private office and invited us in. There were two beautiful Caucasian women sitting there, and chairs had been set up for the rest of us. Dr. Duncan said the women, whom he introduced as Betty Wagner and Muriel Hamlin, were the ones who wanted to meet with us.

Ms. Wagner, whom we soon came to know simply as Betty, addressed us. "I've spoken with Rev. Perkins," she said, "and he explained to us that you kids were having some financial problems." That was the first time I realized I wasn't the only one experiencing financial difficulty.

"We want to do what we can to help," Betty continued. "We're going to work with the school to see what the needs are, and we'll take care of the balances."

At the end of the meeting, when we students had a chance to thank our benefactors, I told them simply, "You are an answer to my prayers."

I can't begin to describe the relief and gratitude I felt at that moment. The generosity of these women was truly a blessing from God, and we also took it as confirmation that we were where we were supposed to be.

That day marked the beginning of wonderful relationships with Betty and Muriel. While we were in school, both of these ladies would write to us, send us birthday gifts, and take us out to dinner. Betty even invited us to her home so we could get off campus for a little while. Later, they sent cards and gifts to our children. Betty has visited us in Mississippi, and we try to see her whenever we're in California. Neither of these women has biological children of her own, but both of them have honorary children and grandchildren all around the world because of their willingness to be used by God to help students in need.

Another white woman who reached out to the black students was Ms. Agnes Holt, the campus librarian. She and Rachel became good friends during our freshman year (that summer, Ms. Holt would visit Rachel in Mississippi on her way to Missouri to see her own family). When basketball season started, Ms. Holt offered to give us rides to the away games if we wanted to go. Rachel and I would ride with her to the games, and then we'd stop at a Denny's or somewhere else for dinner with the team on the way back. We'd talk about the game, and the guys would keep us laughing throughout the meal.

LABC's basketball team, and most of the teams we played against, were predominantly white, with only a very few black players. The audiences at the games were likewise primarily white, with a few black family members and students sprinkled among the crowd. As far as I know, there was never a racially motivated fight or other incident at any of the games, but walking into those arenas could be a little intimidating.

Ms. Holt lived in a tiny apartment, but from time to time she would invite all of the black students to come over for a visit. We truly enjoyed and appreciated her hospitality. She also made it a point to encourage the college's administration to invite African Americans to speak at chapel.

These women were truly God-sent, because being a black student at a predominantly white school in the late '60s was not easy. Don't get me wrong. We were grateful that our college experience was free of the violence that accompanied school desegregation in Mississippi. Still, there were some difficult moments.

It was naive of me, but I had arrived at LABC believing everybody would be welcoming. It was a Christian campus, it was California, and the school had approved our applications for admission. I assumed that meant everyone associated with the college wanted us to be there.

I was mistaken.

While many of our fellow students were nice to us, and some were truly glad we were there, there were also those who wanted very little to do with us. I never received any threats, and there weren't any riots, but I did quickly become aware that some of my schoolmates were opposed to certain elements of the Civil Rights Movement.

One time, I noticed a flyer inviting students to come watch a documentary film in the dormitory's lounge, a common area located between the girls' wing and the boys' wing. I was curious, so I went, not having any idea what the film would be about. The lights were darkened, the film began, and soon we were watching clips from Dr. Martin

Luther King's speeches, cut together with footage of various communist leaders, with accompanying commentary accusing Dr. King and his followers of being communists themselves.

The black students who were there got up and walked out. Even though I was surprised and troubled by what had happened, I don't remember complaining about it to the President or anyone else. Rachel, on the other hand, let people know about her displeasure. Outspoken by nature, and extremely intelligent, she was constantly engaging white students in debate, and she always challenged anyone who said something she felt was racist or untrue. Dolphus and Jimmie were also good about speaking out against racist attitudes and propaganda. They didn't get as angry (visibly, anyway) as Rachel did; they would discuss things calmly with people, always trying to both educate and understand them. "Let's talk about it," I would often hear Dolphus say. "Why do you feel that way?"

Coming from Mississippi, I had never related to white people as equals. That combined with a naturally quiet personality and lack of self-confidence made it difficult and frightening for me to challenge white students.

Every once in a while, though, I would be courageous enough to confront someone when I felt they were out of order. I remember one interaction I had with another female student. "Martin Luther King was always talking about nonviolence, but he started more riots than anyone else in the world," she said.

"Dr. King didn't start riots," I told her. "In fact, oftentimes the Blacks involved aren't the instigators of the violence."

The girl disagreed with my assessment, and as she continued to talk, she got louder and more agitated. I quickly gave up arguing with her, and after that, for the most part, I stayed quiet when racial issues came up. It seemed like the people whose opinions differed from mine had already made their minds up, and I wasn't going to get far trying to reason with them. Besides, I was on campus to get an education, not to win arguments with fellow students.

Apparently, though, I was involved in at least one confrontation besides the one I've just described. In the mid-'90s, I received a telephone call from a different former schoolmate. The caller said I had challenged him about something once when we were in school, and now, almost 30 years later, he wanted to apologize for what he had said. I didn't remember the original conversation at all (though when I looked the gentleman up in an old yearbook, he did seem familiar), but I accepted his apology. I was amazed, and touched, that something I had said so long ago would have such an impact on someone I barely knew. And I give that man a lot of credit for going to the effort of finding me and making things right, when it would have been so easy to leave well enough alone.

Sometimes I had trouble distinguishing between racial bias and personality difference. I had a mixed—and confusing—experience with the white roommate I had during my first semester at LABC. She was kind to me and gave me a lot of things—an iron, a lovely blue bedspread to match hers, some clothes—and I appreciated her generosity, because I had very little. But she was also used to speaking her mind, and sometimes I wasn't sure how to interpret the things she said.

One night, I came in late from work, and I turned on the light because I still had studying to do before I went to bed. My roommate was trying to sleep, and she got upset with me for turning on the light. (Later, she did apologize for getting mad and suggested that we pray together.) But then one night, when I had already gone to bed, she invited some friends over to the room, and they stayed up late, talking and laughing loudly. I should have just told them, "I'm trying to sleep," but instead I tossed and turned, waiting for them to get done with their visit. Because I wasn't bold enough to talk to my roommate about what had happened, I'll never know if she felt that she had more right to the room, as a white person, than I did, or if she would have behaved the same way with a white roommate.

I mentioned before that Ms. Holt encouraged the administration to bring black speakers to our daily chapel gatherings. Her efforts bore some fruit, although the number of black speakers invited while I was at the college was fairly small. The first one I remember was Ed Bryant of Pasadena Christian Center. Mr. Bryant ran an excellent youth ministry (several of us later visited him there and saw the work he was doing), and he was a great speaker. As soon as chapel was over that morning, the black students flocked to him, eager to shake his hand and ask him questions.

The hundreds of other chapel speakers we heard from over the years came from many different places, including Bob Jones University. I remember one time, when we knew someone from Bob Jones would be speaking, someone (probably Dolphus or Jimmie) had the idea that all of the black students should sit in the front row. At some point during his message, we would all cross our legs at the same time, trying to distract and unsettle the speaker. Of course, as an adult, I'm aware that this behavior was rather rude, but at the time our goal was to make our presence felt, and I'm pretty sure we did.

Those daily chapel services at LABC were my first opportunities to worship in a predominantly white environment. Chapel was held in the gym; we would all sit in the bleachers on one side, and a podium would be set up on the gym floor. The experience was somewhat uncomfortable at first—I had to get used to a different style of music, different style of preaching, and different style of participating in worship. Eventually, though, I came to appreciate many things about those services, especially the hymns. Many of those songs have stuck with me, and I love singing them to this day.

Although there were challenges involved with being part of an integrating minority group (did I mention that Dolphus and Jimmie had been the first African Americans to enroll full-time at LABC, and that Carolyn, Rachel and I were the college's first black female students?), there was also a special sweetness to relationships we had with people, both white and black, who reached out to us during this time.

For instance, there was a group of girls who lived in the dorm with me during my sophomore year, including my roommate at that time, Karen Aspinall. Growing up, I had never celebrated my birthday, and these girls threw me my first-ever birthday party. It was a surprise—one of the other girls asked me to come to her room for something, and when I returned to my room, quite a few of the young women from the dorm were there. Karen gave me a pretty pink robe, and I was so touched by the kindness and generosity of these new friends that I actually shed a few tears of gratitude.

From time to time, a group of us would go into Los Angeles to visit Dr. and Mrs. S.P. Weathersby, a couple from D'Lo, Mississippi (Dolphus's home town). Dolphus and the

Weathersbys were actually distant relatives. Dr. Weathersby was a veterinarian who worked for the government, inspecting meat, and Mrs. Weathersby was a schoolteacher. They and their children were incredibly hospitable—they assured us we were welcome to visit any time, and they always fed us whenever we came over. Their home was a real haven for us when we needed to get away from campus for a little while.

We had another home away from home in nearby Monrovia. The couple we called "Mama and Papa Wilson" had "adopted" John Perkins when he first moved out to California, and they extended their gracious hospitality to us as well. They'd even let us spend the night at their place if we wanted. Papa was a short guy, and he had been a jockey, so he always had great stories. And Mama Wilson would make delicious tacos for us to enjoy when we visited. We really appreciated the chance to spend time with them—it was good just to relax in the company of other African Americans.

Back on campus, there were also some faculty members who really wanted the black students to succeed. These men, and their wives, made a real effort to reach out to us, both socially and academically. Early in the fall semester of my freshman year, Dr. Patterson (a highly respected professor who taught history, among other things) and his wife invited several of us to their home for dinner. Their kindness was genuine and much appreciated; even so, that first dinner was incredibly awkward for me. The only time I'd been in a white person's home before was as a hired worker, shelling peas. I had never been invited into a white household for a visit, and I had certainly never sat down to eat a meal together with a white family who treated me and my friends as if we were their special guests.

The dinner (pot roast) was delicious, and the portions they served us were huge. After supper, Mrs. Patterson brought out a beautiful lemon pie and cut an enormous slice for each of us. I'd never had a dessert that big. As full as I was, I knew there was no way I could eat the whole thing, but it was so good, I sure wanted to!

Coach Reese and his wife also regularly opened their home to students—they would invite the basketball team and some of their fans over, and Mrs. Reese always made the best pizza. She had to make a lot of it, too, because those guys could really eat.

Then there were Dr. and Mrs. Gruss, and Mr. and Mrs. Hill. Mrs. Gruss made wonderful beef burritos. Mr. and Mrs. Hill always took us out to dinner—I don't know if Mrs. Hill didn't like to cook, or if they just thought we would enjoy getting to eat at some of the local restaurants.

It's interesting to me that with all the things I can't remember from those years, I can recall exactly what these couples served us for dinner. There's something about sharing meals—especially with people you're not accustomed to sharing meals with—that feels very intimate. I might even go so far as to say that food served with kindness nurtures not just the body, but the spirit as well. In any case, we were deeply grateful to these men and women who made us feel welcome and cared for while we were a long way from our homes and families.

Some of the same professors who looked out for us socially also helped me to survive academically. Honestly, I'm not sure how I would have made it through college without them, because I discovered early on that the academic work at

LABC was much, much harder than what I had experienced in high school.

In high school, I had gotten all A's and B's. In college, I got mostly B's and C's, an occasional A, and one D, in psychology. I had never really taken notes in high school. The teachers gave us whatever we needed to study. In college, I was always scribbling furiously in class, and I just never seemed to be able to write fast enough. While I was jotting one thing down, I'd miss something else. So I would have to spend time outside of class trying to fill in my notes before I could even start studying.

As to the material being presented in the lectures, I often didn't understand it, and I didn't know how to ask the right questions to figure things out. I also didn't realize right away that the professors would help me if I asked. So I just struggled through, telling myself frequently, "Girl, you are in trouble!" and asking myself if I had done the right thing—if I was really supposed to be where I was.

I am a morning person by nature, but that first year, I often worked the breakfast shift in the dining hall, then had my classes (and might work lunch or dinner as well). So I would try to do my studying in the evening, when I was so tired that nothing seemed to stick. I would finally give up, go to sleep, and then wake up about 3:00 or 4:00 in the morning, still tired, and study some more. The whole time I was in college, I don't think I ever got enough sleep.

My psychology class was especially difficult. I could barely understand the professor. Then I would study, study, study for the exams, but the tests would have questions about different material on them. "Why should I test you on stuff you already know?" the professor asked us. So I learned that I had to read ahead just to be ready for the exams.

Even in my Bible courses, which I loved, I was playing catch-up. Although I'd gone to Sunday School classes all my life, I discovered that I didn't actually know a lot about the Bible. I was reading constantly, trying to stay afloat.

I heard that the college offered tutoring, but I assumed it cost money, so I didn't take advantage of the service. Years later, I learned that it had been available free of charge.

As I floundered in these difficult academic waters, Dr. Patterson and Mr. Hill threw me lifelines. Dr. Patterson, seeing how I was struggling in his history class, suggested that I stay late, so he could go over the day's lesson again with me. He would explain things, and then ask if I had questions, making sure that I understood the material before he let me leave.

Mr. Hill taught my speech class. His advice was simple, but it made all the difference. "Rosie, you don't have to choose such hard subjects," he told me. "The point of the assignment is to make a good argument. You can do that using a simpler subject." His wisdom stays with me to this day: Sometimes we set ourselves up to fail by making things harder for ourselves than they need to be. Perhaps we can do more excellent work if, even while stepping out in faith and trusting God to do big things beyond our own abilities, we also exercise discernment about the types and sizes of the problems we choose to attack.

So how was it that I found myself in the kind of trouble I faced at LABC? How had I done so well in high school, yet not been prepared for college?

The sad truth is that Mississippi's educational system lags behind most, even today. I'm very grateful for the current emphasis on improving education for our young people, and I have nothing but admiration for the many excellent and hard-working teachers in our state, but you still often hear stories about students who move out-of-state and find themselves behind in their new classes. In the segregated system of the 1960s, black students were even further behind than white students from the state. How could we not be? A lot of what we had in our schools, we got when the white schools were done with them. Textbooks, choir robes, curtains for our stage, and so on—a significant portion of our educational experience consisted of hand-me-downs.

One of the difficult lessons I learned at LABC was that, like many others before and after me, I had gotten out of Mississippi, but I hadn't yet managed to escape the stunting shadows that had hovered over my childhood and youth.

Chapter Two
Growing Up In Shadows: A childhood in rural Mississippi

I've heard some people say that as children they didn't realize they were poor. I suppose I understand that. As a child, especially as a poor child with no television and very few books, you don't have a whole lot to which you can compare your own experience.

Still, I figured out pretty early on that my family was poor. I knew we were poor because while other children ate lunch in the school cafeteria every day, my siblings and I hardly ever did. Sometimes my brothers, who worked odd jobs, would buy their own lunches, and every once in a while, on special occasions, Daddy would scrape together the eight cents per child it took for all of us to eat at school, but those occasions were rare. Because our mother was often unwell, many times we hadn't had breakfast, either. So it wasn't unusual for our first meal of the day to be supper. Some nights, supper included meat or fish, but often the evening meal was very simple. We might have "pot liquor" (the broth left over from cooking greens or other vegetables) and bread. Or biscuits with sugar syrup, which was just sugar and water heated on the stove until it thickened a bit. Cornbread and milk comprised another standard dinner at our house.

I definitely knew we were poor at Christmas-time, when other children talked about the toys they had received as gifts. We would have had a delicious meal, with turkey or chicken, dressing, cakes and pies, and we would have received apples and oranges, maybe some candy or raisins and nuts. But no toys. Many of our schoolmates also received presents on their birthdays, while ours came and went unobserved.

It's funny the way a child's mind conceptualizes wealth. From early on, I dreamed of escaping poverty, and at first my vision was of a day when I would have enough money to go into a store and buy all the cookies I wanted. And clothes. I would be able to buy clothes, rather than wear the floor-length dresses my father's cousin Aquilla made for the girls in our family. (We used our belts to shorten those dresses when our parents weren't looking, incidentally.) Over time, the dream changed, and I began to imagine the possibility of owning the store; of course, as the owner, I would be able to eat as many cookies as my heart desired.

In an odd way, my job at the college dining hall—a position generally considered menial—fulfilled this childhood dream. No, I didn't own anything, but for the first time in my life, I had consistent access to food that was both varied and plentiful. I still remember how luxurious it felt to be able to eat cookies, or cheese, or whatever else appealed to me, until I'd had enough.

During my teenage years, my dream fell into line with the fantasies of so many young Mississippians: "Making it" was defined simply as getting out of, and far away from, our home state. Later on, I would learn from Rev. Perkins that for some, the dream quickly became a nightmare. When he was volunteering at youth detention centers in southern California, Rev. Perkins encountered many young men who had grown up in the South and left to go looking for success. Often lacking the education and skills they needed to get jobs that would support the lifestyles they desired, their desperation had led to various types of criminal activity.

But as a young person growing up in Mississippi, I had only sunny visions of distant places. I set my sights on escape and kept them there.

Despite my fervent desire to leave it all behind me, my childhood, like most people's childhoods, was a mixture of good and bad, helpful and hurtful experiences and realities. Understanding how both the positive and the negative have affected me is a process that continues to this day.

My parents, Ernest and Rosie (Brown) Camper, were farmers. They grew cotton, corn, cucumbers, sweet potatoes, sugar cane and other crops on about 25 of the 80 acres of land that belonged to Daddy's family. When I was in high school, Daddy finally got clear title to most of this land, but while I was a child, it was still "heir land," so any income from timber or leasing had to be divided among my father and his siblings.

My parents raised livestock (pigs, cows and chicken), and they also made their own corn meal and syrup. This meant they only ever had to go to the store for a few staples—flour, salt, sugar and the like. They were independent, self-sufficient, and stoic, rarely showing much emotion toward each other or their children. Although I don't remember them ever hugging us or telling us they loved us, I'm sure they did love us. It was the kind of love that demonstrates itself in hard work, provision and presence rather than through expressions of affection.

Like many family farmers who needed plenty of hands to do the work, my parents had quite a few children, ten to be exact (three boys and seven girls). We Camper kids are like stair-steps, born one after another. I am number six.

We also had a half-brother, M.B., who was our father's child from a previous relationship. M.B. didn't live with us, but one of my earliest memories is of him picking me up and playing with me while he was visiting our father. M.B. drifted in and out of our lives over the years. At one point, he and his mother lived just down the road from us (I imagine this was probably a little awkward for *my* mother, although I don't remember her saying so), and M.B. would stop by from time to time. There were also long stretches when we didn't see him at all, including when he lived in Michigan for a while. Although he didn't talk or look like our father, M.B. had Daddy's sense of humor—the two of them (and my sister, Esta, too) could always keep the rest of us in stitches.

Most of my very early memories center around my mother. Mama was light-skinned, tall (she was just a little bit taller than Daddy, which may be why she rarely wore high heels) and slightly overweight. She was meticulous about her hygiene, keeping herself and her clothes neat and clean, and always powdering her face and doing her hair before she went out in public. Children in the community were drawn to my mother and loved hanging out at our house.

Part of the reason for that was that Mama was one of the best cooks around. "She could make gravy taste good" was the way some people put it. (That saying seems rather odd to me now, as my experience has been that gravy tastes good more often than not, but it's what I remember hearing people say.) Everybody in the community loved her food, and Mama, who always wanted to please people, loved their compliments.

Consequently, most of the opportunities we kids had to spend time with Mama involved helping her in the kitchen. I always looked forward to those times, partly because I wanted to lick the bowls when she baked, and partly because I enjoyed being around my mother and trying to be like her. I would wear an apron, just like she did, and she'd give instructions as we went along. She might let me beat the eggs, or measure some of the ingredients for a cake. (She measured only when she was making a cake; everything else, she did by estimating and tasting. To this day, I cook the same way, which is why I can't give people my recipes when they ask for them. I just keep at it until the food tastes right.) Sometimes Mama would send me to fetch greens from the garden and wash them—and keep washing them, because it's not easy to get all the dirt out of greens.

We didn't have a can opener, so when we needed to open a can (of evaporated milk, for instance), we took a knife and beat down on the lid with it. Even though I now own two or three can openers (including an electric one), I still open cans this way. So do my sisters. When Dolphus and I were in Africa recently, a woman brought out a can of milk for our coffee. She picked up a knife, and I thought, "Surely she's not…" But she did. She opened the can exactly the same way my mother used to do it.

Mama made amazing tea cakes (a legacy that has become part of my ministry over the years) and delicious fruit jellies. I remember picking peaches and plums when it was jelly-making time. Then, while my siblings and I washed the fruit, our mother would not only teach us cooking skills, but also drill other lessons into us.

One of her favorites was the value of cleanliness. "Cleanliness is next to godliness," she always said, and if that's true, then my mother's house was a very godly place. Her mother was the same way, and I suspect that they were both reacting to the stereotype many white people held at the time: that Blacks were dirty, stupid, etc. My mother only had a seventh or eighth grade education, but she wasn't stupid, and she definitely wasn't dirty. I think she wanted to prove that even though she didn't have much in the way of wealth, possessions or a fancy house, she could take good care of what she did have, and she wasn't going to settle for anything less than excellence when it came to matters she could control.

Even though our house was always immaculate, twice every year it got even cleaner. We kids dreaded these major cleaning events, which lasted two or three days each time. From sweeping and dusting the attic, to cleaning the windows and washing the walls, to taking apart and washing the cotton mattresses (this was the chore I hated the most!), we had to help with every kind of cleaning task there was.

Mama's insistence on cleanliness didn't stop at the front door. We also had to cut brush brooms from the dogwood trees so we could clean the yards. That included crawling under the house (where chickens ran rampant) to sweep. And once we moved to our new house, which sat next to an old graveyard where some of our relatives were buried, Mama also made us tidy up the graves and cut the grass with sling blades. (For anyone who hasn't ever encountered a sling blade, it's a sharp double blade attached to a wooden handle about three feet long. In order to cut grass or weeds with it, you hold it out in front of you and swing it from side to side. It's exhausting work, especially when you're a child with short arms!)

My siblings and I did manage to find a few ways to make the spring and fall cleanings less miserable. Since we heated wash water over an outdoor fire, we could grab some sweet potatoes from the sweet potato bank (a tiny wooden "house" in the back yard where the potatoes were stored covered in straw so they wouldn't rot) and stick them in the coals to bake while we waited for the water to get hot. They wouldn't cook completely, but they still made for a tasty snack and a welcome break from chores. When we went out to get the brush brooms, that also gave us a chance to gather hickory nuts, which my brothers would crack open with hammers so we could eat them.

Mama basically operated in two modes: sick in bed and perpetual motion. If she was well enough to be up and about, she was sure to be busy. When she wasn't making her own lye soap, washing clothes three times a week, hanging them on a line to dry, ironing with a metal iron heated on the stove, preparing meals, preserving meats and fruits, making butter, or tending her flower and vegetable gardens, she was fussing over our hair. Like her part-Native American mother, Mama and her girls all had long hair, and that hair was her pride and joy. She went to great lengths to keep our hair looking nice, always combing it and making sure it was clean. She was an expert with regard to hair products, and for a while she sold E.F. Young products (like tar shampoo, hair pomade, and wax for men to use to make their hair wavy) for supplemental income. Her children were her staff—we would walk from house to house, delivering orders to her customers.

Mama's mother, Minnie Carter Brown, lived up the road on a hill, and she was constantly working in her garden, which was filled with beautiful flowers. Grandma Minnie had one of the fiercest barks I've ever heard. Fortunately for us kids, her bite was much less serious. I wouldn't want to repeat the things she used to say to us, but her utterances often started with, "If my hand wasn't hurting..." and concluded with various threats. The funny thing was, while Grandma Minnie's hand always seemed to be in too much pain to discipline her grandchildren, it would be healthy enough to hoe her garden just minutes later. So we didn't let her yelling worry us too much. Like my parents, while Grandma Minnie wasn't very affectionate, she would do anything she could to help out when there was a need. I remember one time, when my father didn't have any money except one silver dollar, Grandma

Minnie let him "pawn" that silver dollar to her for a paper bill and then buy it back later.

Grandma Minnie never told my mother who her (that is to say, Mama's) father was; three men claimed her as their daughter, but Minnie denied each claim. She got married when my mother was a teenager, but her husband was out of the picture by the time I was born, and I never met him. Besides my mother, Grandma Minnie also had an informally adopted son, Carvell (called Bob), who was hard to understand because of a severe stutter. I don't know anything about Bob's birth family, or how Grandma Minnie ended up getting him, but I know she raised Bob from a small child, and she loved him dearly. Sometimes, I have to say, it seemed like she cared for Bob more than she did for Mama. At one point, Grandma Minnie deeded a portion of her land to Bob; she didn't give any to my mother, who had plowed that land as a girl (hard work that fell to her because she didn't have brothers or a father in the home). Mama didn't want to do anything while Grandma Minnie was still living, but she told us kids that we needed to make sure, when Grandma Minnie died, that the rest of the land stayed in our family.

A highly superstitious woman, Grandma Minnie periodically consulted fortune tellers and always wore a rabbit's foot around her neck for luck. One time, a woman who had come from Seattle to volunteer with The Mendenhall Ministries visited my grandmother at her home and started to share Christ with her. Grandma Minnie pulled that rabbit's foot out from under her shirt and said, "This is all I need!" It broke my heart when the volunteer told me that. When she was sick in the hospital, though, you could hear Grandma Minnie all the way down the hall, calling out, "Oh, Lordy,

Lordy." My prayer is that she really did cry out to the Lord in her last days and put her trust in him.

While Mama could be firm with us kids about what she expected of us, she was timid in most other contexts, including relating to Daddy. Generally, my parents got along well enough (they were civil and respectful, if not affectionate, toward each other), but I always hated to see the holidays come, because that's when you could count on there being tension between them. Mama would want to change something around the house to liven things up (maybe put new curtains up, replace the linoleum in the kitchen, or get a new spread for their bed), but Daddy would say it wasn't necessary, and besides, we didn't have the money. He was frugal, almost to the point of stinginess. And Mama, even when she didn't agree with him, would bottle up her feelings and hold them inside. At least, she bottled them up in front of Daddy. We kids would see her crying, and she would often confide in my sister Earlene about her frustration and disappointment. It always made me sad to think about the things she wanted but didn't have—in part because she wasn't willing or able to stand up for herself.

This trait is one that I inherited from her, and that I would spend many years and much heartache battling later in my life.

My father was a handsome man who, like Mama, paid careful attention to his appearance. He dressed neatly and almost always wore a hat (a fedora, I think it was called). He kept his hair dyed as long as he had a full head of it; when it started to thin, he shaved his head. He was slim, darker-skinned than my mother, and athletic. In fact, many people said that Daddy could have played professional baseball, if

Major League Baseball had been integrated back then. (Communication then not being what it is today, I'm not sure if people in our community even knew about the Negro Leagues.) To tell the truth, I don't remember Daddy talking about wanting to be a professional baseball player, although I do remember him playing catch with us kids and coaching a little now and then. He also taught my brothers how to hunt (they brought home rabbits, squirrels, raccoons, beavers and turtles—all of which we ate), and of course he taught all of us how to farm.

Because on a family farm, everybody works, even the smallest children. For a long time, I thought okra plants were very tall, like trees. Eventually, I realized it wasn't that they were so tall, it was that I was still very short when I used to be sent into the garden after okra, or greens—which I learned to tell apart from each other at a young age. We kids sowed fertilizer, dropped corn and peas, carried water, helped feed the animals, shucked corn, gathered wood for the heater, and fished, mostly for brim and catfish. One of my assigned chores was milking the cows, which meant getting up in the wee hours of the morning. To this day, I am an early riser—I guess it feels natural to start my day well before sunup.

The fishing was the part I loved the best. We used cane poles, and we would dig up earthworms for bait, then run down to the creek and see if the fish were biting that day. Sometimes we'd catch something, sometimes we wouldn't, but either way, I loved being by the water. I'm the kind of person who can sit out all day, never get a bite, and still enjoy myself. Not that I had that luxury as a child, of course—fishing then was a matter of subsistence, not recreation.

As we got older, we graduated to more strenuous jobs, like picking cucumbers. Now, if you didn't grow up on a farm, picking cucumbers might not sound like hard work, but trust me, it is. Because the vines grow low to the ground, you have to bend over to do the picking (you can't sit or squat because of how densely the vines cover the ground). So your back starts aching pretty quickly. Then, once you've picked all the cucumbers you can see, you have to raise the vines to make sure you've gotten all the ones growing underneath. In the process, your hands turn black from the sticky residue that covers them. Picking cucumbers was tedious, exhausting and painful, but since it was the one thing around the farm that Daddy paid us to do, I guess I'm glad he always kept a half-acre or so planted with them.

As farmers, we were surrounded by food, but that didn't mean we always ate well. Farming is seasonal, so between harvests, we had to ration our use of preserved foods carefully. You certainly couldn't have called our diet balanced. And every once in a while, we came close to not having any supper at all. I remember one of those times as clearly as if it were yesterday.

"I've got a little cornmeal, but nothing else," Mama told us that afternoon. "Can you kids try and catch some fish so we can have something to eat?"

I don't remember her seeming upset, but I'm sure it was a burden for her—no parent wants their kids to go hungry, and a little cornmeal wasn't going to go far toward satisfying the appetites of ten children (not to mention two hard-working adults).

As it turned out, my brothers managed to catch quite a few fish, and we had a very nice supper that night. In fact, in my memory, that's the best cornbread and fish I've ever eaten, probably because it's so clear in retrospect that God provided it for us.

Daddy was an incredibly hard worker and disciplined human being, and he expected no less from his children. He insisted that, in addition to doing our chores, we study hard and do our homework, and it was very difficult to get away with anything when he was around. I only remember him spanking me once—most of the time, he just had to speak to command respect and instant obedience. I never rode the school-bus Daddy drove later on, but I'm sure the kids who did ride it were well-behaved!

There was one rule we broke on a regular basis: Daddy's prohibition against playing cards. He thought cards were of the devil, and he forbade us to have anything to do with them. But somehow we'd gotten hold of a deck, and we figured out how to play without getting caught. We'd simply wait until Daddy was dozing on the back porch, and then we'd set up our game—Casino, Pit-a-pat, Smuts and I don't remember what else—on the front porch. We'd be able to hear him when he opened the screen door from the back porch and began walking down the hallway.

"He's coming, he's coming," we'd whisper, and one of my sisters would quickly hide the deck of cards before Daddy got to where we were.

One time, we were playing while a storm was brewing. All of a sudden, there was a flash of lightning so close we felt the heat on our cheeks. Then the thunder clap came right away, loud, like a shotgun fired right over our heads. We ran back into the house, terrified and wondering if Daddy had been right all along. The next morning, we saw that the lightning had struck and splintered a huge tree in our backyard. I have one sister who has never played cards since that day!

In addition to cards, we kids found all sorts of other ways to entertain ourselves. The only store-bought toys I remember us having were dominoes and marbles (which we shot for keeps). To supplement our toy collection, we made Jacob's Ladders with string, and my brothers got creative with the leather scraps, old tires and sticks they found lying around, manufacturing slingshots, bows and arrows, and even wagons.

Mostly, though, we played games. Hide and seek, "Little Sally Walker," and other circle games, some of which we learned and some of which we made up ourselves. And mud cakes. We loved making mud cakes, mashing up berries for icing until our fingernails were completely red.

Sometimes, when we'd finished our schoolwork and chores, we were allowed to go to Cousin Aquilla's house to watch television. Aquilla was the first person in our community to own a television, so we thought we were pretty special, getting to visit her and watch the shows that appeared on the screen as if by magic.

A wonderful person who loved the Lord, Aquilla was truly a blessing, not only to her own family, but to our whole community. She worked at the YMCA camp in Pinola. Blacks weren't allowed to attend activities there at that time, but she would often bring home leftover food from events and share it with our family. Aquilla's husband had been in the military, and after he died, she started receiving a check every month. She never used that money all for herself; she always shared what she'd been given with others who were in need.

Aquilla really loved young people, but she didn't have any children of her own, and all of her nieces and nephews lived far away. When my youngest sister, Sandra (whom we called San), was born, Aquilla asked Mama if she could adopt her. Mama said no, of course. Later on, whenever Aquilla came to our house to visit, she would wear her apron with the big pockets. In those pockets were goodies for San, who would then want to go home with Aquilla. Eventually, Mama's resistance wore down, and she said San could stay with Aquilla (who only lived a couple of houses away from us).

As much as I enjoyed playing with my brothers and sisters or going to Cousin Aquilla's house, I also cherished moments of solitude. Sometimes when it rained, I would lie down in the hallway and listen to the drops falling on our tin roof. When the weather was nice, I'd often climb one of the persimmon trees in our yard, sit among the branches, and spend hours dreaming about getting out of poverty.

Sadly, my father's parents, Janie and Walt Camper, were only part of my life for a very short time. As a little girl, I thought Grandma Janie was the meanest person in the world, because she wouldn't play with us kids. Instead, she gave us warm Kool-Aid (which we called "soft drink" back then), and she wiped the pickles from the pickle jar with a dishrag before handing them to us. I wish I'd gotten the chance to see her through something other than a child's perspective, but she died when I was very young (before I'd even started school). Grandpa Walt was an extremely frugal man; he hated to waste anything, or really even to spend money at all. So my father came by that personality trait honestly!

I don't remember Grandma Janie ever coming to visit us at our house across the creek, although I imagine she probably did. I do remember bald-headed Grandpa Walt's visits. Mama gave him hot cornbread and butter whenever he came over—I don't know if that's *why* he came to visit, but he certainly enjoyed the food. After Grandma Janie died, Grandpa Walt lived by himself for a while. Not too much later, though, he got sick with kidney problems, and he went to stay with my Aunt Nola and Uncle Ike, since most of their children were already grown and out of the house.

Daddy drove Grandpa's old Ford to my aunt's house just about every day to draw fluid off of Grandpa Walt while he was sick. Sometimes we kids would ride along, but we'd stay in the car or play outside while Daddy went in to tend to his father. All of this happened while I was still young enough that as we'd bump along the road in that old car, I thought the trees were moving in the opposite direction.

In those days, black folks hardly ever went to the doctor unless it was an emergency, for a number of reasons. For one thing, why would you spend precious money on a doctor's visit when there was a home remedy for just about every ailment? A polk salad leaf on the head or stomach took care of a fever; castor oil (terrible stuff!), 366 cold medicine, and tallow on our chests cured colds; spider webs or chimney smut stopped the bleeding when we got cuts; and if you were unfortunate enough to be stung by a wasp, you would rub snuff on the wound.

Even the births of children generally happened at home. I was too young when my sisters Esta and Eula were born to remember anything, but I do recall the day Elizabeth was born. We kids were sent outside to play while two midwives boiled water and attended our mother. When we were allowed back in the house, the first thing we heard was a baby crying.

"Where did that baby come from?" I asked.

Mama replied, "The midwives brought her." That puzzled me, because I had seen the midwives arrive earlier in the day, and it didn't seem like they had a baby with them then.

Of all Mama's children, Sandra is the only one who was born at a hospital. Again, I didn't know Mama was pregnant; she just went off to the hospital and came back with a baby.

These things remained mysterious to me until our high school biology teacher taught us about human reproduction. One of the things I learned in that class was that pregnancy tests were sometimes called "rabbit tests," at least when the person being tested was a young, black female. Which brings us to another reason that many Blacks were hesitant to seek medical attention in those days…

The first time I ever went to a doctor was when I was in the eleventh grade. I had been having what we referred to simply as "female problems," so my parents took me to a clinic in Crystal Springs. The doctor asked a couple of questions, then instructed the nurse to give me a rabbit test.

"I am not pregnant," I said indignantly, offended that the doctor just assumed I was sexually active, especially since my symptoms weren't even consistent with pregnancy.

The doctor and nurse both turned red (I guess they hadn't expected me to know what they were talking about), but they proceeded with the test anyway. "You're not pregnant," the doctor announced, unnecessarily, when he returned to the exam room.

Then he gave me a shot of something without telling me what it was. Mama, Daddy and I walked out to the car, and I remember falling, then waking up back in the doctor's office. He asked me a few more questions, decided that I had "gotten too hot," and sent me home. The shot did not resolve my health problems, but even so, I didn't see a doctor again until I needed pre-marital blood tests three years later.

Throughout our childhood, Daddy took us kids to church and Sunday School every week. Our church, New Zion Baptist, was a very emotional place, with lots of shouting. Only many years later, after I'd accepted Christ as my personal savior, did I realize that you didn't have to shout to be a Christian. Our pastor served several congregations, so he only preached at our church once a month. The weeks he wasn't there, we just had Sunday School, where I remember Miss Laurinda Walker teaching us Bible stories, but I don't remember learning about salvation or the need for a personal relationship with Christ.

Her poor health and frequent pregnancies prevented Mama from coming to church with us very often. As reserved as she was, when she did come, she didn't worship enthusiastically (that is to say, shout) the way most of the other ladies did. Because of those things, there were times when I thought maybe she wasn't a Christian. Then again, she was the one who gave us kids pocket New Testaments to read. "Go look at the sun as it rises, and read your Bibles," she told us. With that simple instruction, she taught us to learn about God through both His Word and His creation.

For a child, coming to church could be something of a mixed blessing. On one hand, every woman there was like a surrogate mother, able to discipline you for any infraction, real or suspected. On the other hand, Mr. Bill McLaurin was always there with a pocketful of peppermint candies that he'd hand out to a few lucky children each week. While our church didn't have a formal children's ministry, there were roles young people could fill—you could be Sunday School secretary, or a convention delegate (a role that marked the beginning of my journey to California, as you may recall).

The New Zion Baptist Church of my growing-up years didn't particularly look like a church from the outside. It was a plain white, wood-sided building, with no stained glass or steeple. Inside, I remember there being stairs everywhere. Stairs up from the entryway to the main level, more stairs to the pulpit and around it to the choir stand, another flight to the Sunday School rooms, each with beautiful wood railings. The wood benches were less beautiful, and not at all comfortable, but even so, I apparently managed to doze off from time to time while sitting on them. I remember Mama, on some of the rare occasions when she attended service with us, waking me up when I'd fallen asleep. At our church, as in many at that time, the men sat on one side of the sanctuary, while the women sat on the other. The young people generally sat somewhere in the middle, and up front was the "Amen Corner" where the "more spiritual" people sat.

When revival time came, it was like a big family reunion, and everybody pitched in. We'd gather beforehand to clean the church; everything had to be just right when visitors were coming. During the revival itself, people brought big boxes of food, and they'd serve plates from the backs of pickups and the trunks of cars. I always got my plate from Mama's station: chicken and dumplings or her renowned cornflake-crusted fried chicken, cornbread dressing, potato pie… Someone would always bring a big drum of the most delicious lemonade. Cousin Aquilla would make her famous egg pies, and Mrs. Dora Walker would have some sort of cake or another with a split down the middle. "It ain't good unless it's split," she always said.

Along the road leading to the church, vendors would set up shop, selling peanuts, snow cones and other treats. The peanut vendor was a gentleman we called Mr. Blind Red. Although he couldn't see, Blind Red sure could count money. From time to time, someone would try to cheat him, but he always knew.

When I was four years old or so, Daddy had a new house built for us on the Pinola-Braxton road. People had been encouraging him to move for some time—our old house was in the woods, there was only one other house in the area, and it really wasn't safe for the kids to be walking back and forth across the creek. The new house was about half a mile away from the old one, and we did still go back and forth a lot—to maintain the farm, to carry water from the well, and so on.

Now, when I say we had a new house, people sometimes get the wrong impression. There was nothing fancy about this house. It had two bedrooms—one for the boys, and one for the girls. The girls' room had a double bed and a cot in it. Two of my sisters shared the cot, while the rest of us piled into the bed. There was no space for any other furniture in that room. To give you another way to understand its size, after all the kids were grown, and Mama and Daddy finally got indoor plumbing in the house, they turned the girls' bedroom into their bathroom. Between the two bedrooms, there was a little closet; Mama would fold all of our clothes and pile them on a shelf in the closet, stacked almost all the way to the ceiling. When you needed to find something to wear, you'd look through the pile and then pull your clothes out carefully, trying not to cause the stack to fall and scatter clothes all over the place.

Mama and Daddy slept in the family room, where the wood heater was. There was also a dining room (too tiny for a table the whole family could sit around), a kitchen and a small living room. There were holes in that house, and no insulation, so the wind blew right in. In winter, it got so cold inside, I didn't think I'd ever get warm again. Mama would cover us kids up with old coats at night to try to keep us warm. In the summer, it was the opposite—miserably hot. We didn't have any fans, so we kept the windows up to try to get a breeze going. To keep the mosquitoes away, we burned old rags, or diesel from the railroad tracks.

As I already mentioned, our house had no indoor plumbing, so besides the well water we carried over from the farm for drinking and cooking, we also set drums out to catch rainwater for bathing. We bathed in a No. 2 washtub. Each batch of water that Mama heated on the wood-burning stove was good for three kids to use, one after the other, in order of age.

One of the nice things about our house was the back porch. In the summer, when it was too hot to go to bed, we'd sit out there and sing songs, while my brothers played on guitars they'd made from boards, nails and wires. I especially remember all of us singing "O Come Over Here," about the table being spread for the feast of the Lord.

One of the not-so-nice things about the new house was how close it was to a graveyard. When you went out our back door, there it was, and since there were no electric lights, it would be pitch dark except for maybe a little bit of moonlight. My brothers and cousins loved to tell us younger kids stories about the "haints," as they called them. They spoke of headless ghosts walking down the road, then disappearing into thin air. It was especially scary when someone in the community had died recently—it was so easy to think you saw a familiar figure in the shadows. More than once, when the stories started, I ran back into the house, jumped into bed, and pulled the covers up over my head.

Moving across the creek put us significantly closer to the town of Pinola, in access if not in distance. Even though it was a small town (the population was less than 500), Pinola was a bustling place—home to a cotton gin, a cucumber vat (where the cucumbers were graded according to size, smaller being better), three mercantile stores, and a Laundromat. Pinola's population was split fairly evenly between black folks and white folks, and those populations were strictly segregated.

It was after we moved that I began to become aware of the deep divide between the races in our community. Both Blacks and Whites traveled the road on which we now lived, which was the dirt highway connecting Pinola with Harrisville. Every morning, a truckload of young white men drove by our house, and as they did, they shouted racial slurs at the children they passed. My brothers, who were older and more world-wise than I, would yell back, "Hey, you peckerwoods!"

I had no idea what peckerwoods were, so I asked my brothers about it, and they told me it was a term for poor whites.

Our parents had taught us early on to say "yes, sir" and "yes, ma'am" to white folks, and that was about all I knew about dealing with them. I knew we didn't attend the same schools, and since it had always been that way, that's the way I thought it was supposed to be.

When I started school, the year after our move, I learned a thing or two about what "separate but equal" meant when it came to schooling for black and white children in rural Mississippi. While many of the white students rode in shiny yellow school buses that glided quietly down the road and picked them up at their front doors, I had to walk a quarter of a mile to catch the black students' bus. The roads were muddy, I didn't have gloves, and some winter mornings I was really afraid I was going to freeze to death. You could always hear our bus coming, rattling and banging as it approached. Faded yellow in color, it had no heat (I don't know for sure that the white kids' bus had heat, but I heard that it did), and the interior was old and raggedy.

That bus took me to New Hymn High School, which was located about seven miles outside of town (as opposed to the white school, which sat squarely in the middle of Pinola) and served all grades from pre-primer through twelfth. When I first started at New Hymn, the school was made up of one long building on one side of the highway and a smaller classroom building on the other side. Junior high and high school students had to walk across the highway to get to some of their classes. There were no inside facilities, just outhouses. A few years after I started at the school, we got a new building. This one had indoor plumbing and a gym, which meant our basketball team wouldn't have to play their home games on outdoor courts any more.

I had been so excited to start school! I could hardly wait—until I got on the bus that first day. As we bumped along the road, it finally hit me that going to school meant being separated from Mama. I hated being apart from her; I even cried when she left me with Grandma Minnie so she could go into town to run errands. This was even scarier, as I had no idea what to expect, and I cried for the better part of a week. My pre-primer teacher, Mrs. Anna Taylor, tried to comfort me at first, but since she had other students to attend to as well, after a while she had to just let me cry until I got over it.

Part of what captured my attention in the classroom (and distracted me from my distress at being away from home) was the chance to learn how to read. I had heard my sisters read the "Dick and Jane" books to my parents so many times I had them memorized. I could look at the picture on the page, figure out where we were in the story, and say the words that went with that picture, so at first Mrs. Taylor thought I already knew how to read. I didn't, but I picked it up quickly. By the time I started first grade with Mrs. Ola Bell Smith, I was doing so well in my schoolwork that they sent me on to the second grade after just a few weeks. That put me in class with my sister, Earlene, but she was a good student, too, and she got bumped up to third grade shortly after that.

Since school desegregation didn't come to Mississippi until two years after I graduated from high school, I never had a white classmate, or a white teacher, until I went off to college. While there were certainly downsides to being excluded from the white education system, with its more abundant resources, there was an upside as well. Our teachers were black men and women who served as positive role models for young people in our community. They also cared deeply about us and our educations. That didn't mean they wouldn't give us whippings in school—these teachers didn't play—but they loved us and truly wanted to see us excel.

Even though I only spent a short time in Mrs. Smith's classroom, she was impressed with me; she often told me she was proud of me and exhorted me to keep up the good work.

Married but childless, Mrs. Smith often invited girls from the community to come stay with her and her husband for maybe a week at a time over the summer. I was one of the girls she welcomed into her home. Her husband, who called me Rose Marie, thought highly of me as well. I remember Mrs. Smith telling me, "We'd ask your mom if we could adopt you, except we know she'd say no."

Mr. Smith died while I was in high school. When we found out he was sick, students began pouring into the school office and calling the hospital. I remember hearing our principal apologize to Mrs. Smith once for all the disturbances. "They're just worried about him," he explained. I kept in touch with Mrs. Smith even after I'd gone off to (and graduated from) college. One time when I was visiting, Mrs. Smith said to the young lady who was staying with her then, "Why don't you be more like Marie?" I cringed inside, thinking about how that must have made the other girl feel. At the same time, I have to admit it was nice to know that someone who had been so important in my life still had such a good opinion of me.

During my high school years, I had other teachers who took a special interest in me. Mrs. Aletha Parker, who taught history, was a very spiritual lady. Like Mrs. Smith, she was married, but didn't have any children of her own, although she did have nieces whom she kept at least part of the time. Mrs. Parker often talked to me about the Lord. "He'll help you through it, Rosie," she used to say. It seemed like Mrs. Parker could see good things in me that I wasn't yet able to see myself. "You have so much potential. You just need to do your best, and trust Him."

Then there was Miss Fannie McCall, our English teacher. Miss McCall couldn't see well (she used a magnifying glass to read our papers), but she had a keen sense of smell, she was quite strict, and she was determined to get her students to do their very best. If I got a B+ or even an A- on an assignment, I could expect to hear something along the lines of: "Now, Camper, I expect more from you" or "You know that's not the best you can do."

My typing teacher, Mrs. Minley, was also quite good. She was always encouraging (as opposed to other typing teachers I've heard of, who hit your fingers if you messed up), and I credit her for my ability to type proficiently—a skill that has served me well throughout my education and professional life.

When I first started school, our principal was a light-skinned man who didn't seem to care much for darker-skinned people. He wasn't at the school very long. Our next principal was Mr. Gray, and he stayed the whole rest of the time I was at New Hymn. Like my mother, Mr. Gray was a stickler for cleanliness, ensuring that the facilities were kept in tip-top condition, including having our hallways and the gym floor waxed frequently. The County Superintendent, a white man, often bragged publicly about how clean our school was.

To be honest, I don't know how good Mr. Gray was in terms of academics, and I do know that he wasn't a strong disciplinarian. In fact, he reminded me a little of my Grandma Minnie that way. He often threatened to punish students, but he rarely did. As a result, many students didn't respect his authority.

On the other hand, Mr. Gray helped a lot of kids. He told me about the scholarship opportunity at Alcorn and helped me complete my application, and I know I'm not the only one he encouraged and assisted in a college application process. Most of his students were poor, with parents who didn't have much education. Without Mr. Gray, I'm sure many of us wouldn't have realized what options we had, or known how to pursue futures beyond what we had known growing up.

It's amazing how different things look as you get some distance from them. For many years, I tended to be ungrateful, focusing almost exclusively on the negative aspects of my childhood. I thought about all the things we didn't have, and all the ways it was hard to grow up as we did. When I was close to it, I couldn't recognize how blessed we were. Now, I see the ways that God protected us and provided for us, and I've stopped dwelling on the things we lacked—things that, as it turns out, didn't matter nearly as much as the things we did have: shelter, food and people—inside and outside of our immediate family—who cared about us, nurtured us, and invested themselves in our success.

For Mama and Daddy, one of the primary measures of success for their children was that we should all graduate from high school. They made sure we did our homework, and they even sent us to school a few days in September and October. Some black children didn't go to school at all during those months—they were too busy working for the white farmers as well as helping to harvest their own families' corn and sweet potatoes. My parents achieved their goal: All ten of their children finished high school, and several of us went on to college, although I'm the only one who got a degree.

As my high school commencement ceremony approached, my excitement grew by the minute. I felt a huge sense of accomplishment, since many people in our community didn't graduate, and I could hardly wait to go on to college.

My friend, Carolyn, was the valedictorian of our graduating class. Carolyn and I had gone through school together, and I had always figured I should look at the smartest person in the class and try to do better. That person was Carolyn. I'd never quite been able to beat her, but I came close: I was our class salutatorian, graduating with the second highest academic marks.

As the salutatorian, I had to make a speech at the graduation ceremony. I worked terribly hard writing and memorizing that speech. My English teacher, Miss McCall, helped me, and you know if she was involved, it was going to be good. But I set my sights even higher than that. I wanted everything about that day—and especially my speech—to be perfect. Mama didn't come to the ceremony (my parents didn't attend many functions, so this wasn't unusual behavior or anything I took personally), but Daddy was there, along with the County Superintendent and a whole lot of other people. I had planned to take a written copy of my speech onstage with me, just in case, but for reasons I can't recall, I didn't. Partway through, my mind went blank. Completely blank. For the life of me, I could not remember what came next.

The pause probably wasn't that long, but it felt like forever to me. Eventually, I remembered the next line of the speech, and I made it through to the end without any other mistakes. Carolyn came after me and delivered her speech flawlessly, of course.

After the ceremony, Coach Fritz came up to me to congratulate me on my speech and tell me what a good job I'd done. I couldn't even thank him for his kind words. I just walked away and started crying, knowing I had messed up.

That graduation speech was just one of many public speaking traumas in my life, but we'll talk more about that later.

My relationship with my sister Earlene was a lot like Carolyn's and my friendship—close, but with a competitive side. Earlene and I were both cheerleaders, and we did a lot of things together. For instance, when Earlene went on a date, I went, too. Earlene was a drum majorette, and she was pretty and popular, so she went on plenty of dates. She and Esta both did.

I was very shy, so I didn't have much in the way of dates of my own. There was the Fourth of July when I went to Sophia Sutton (a black church-operated retreat center where there were a lot of activities for young people) with a boy from my class, but I spent the whole time wishing I had gone with my sister instead. There was another young man who liked me, but we never really dated, either, just went to one party together. Boys weren't really my thing—it was all about doing well in school and preparing for a successful future.

Earlene and I were about the same size, so we wore each other's clothes a lot. One time, she wore a new dress of mine to school, before I'd even gotten a chance to wear it. Several of her classmates complimented her on it, but she shrugged off their praise.

"I don't really like it that much," she said nonchalantly. "I'm probably going to give it to Rosie."

The first time I wore the dress, people told me how nice Earlene was to have given it to me. Of course, their comments annoyed me, but as it turned out, that dress was about to spark a new dream for my future.

I can still picture it: brown plaid skirt, brown floral and plaid print top, with a belt in between. A girl who was studying home economics approached me. "You know," she said thoughtfully, "ordinarily those two patterns wouldn't match, but it's okay because you've got the same color and pattern above and below the belt."

Before that day, nobody had ever said anything to me about things matching. As I thought about what this girl had said, I started thinking about clothing more generally, and I began to dream about the possibility of becoming a fashion model.

My oldest sister had moved to Jackson, and one time when I was visiting her, I saw a magazine she had. In this magazine were pictures of a beautiful black woman named Naomi Sims modeling clothes, and I decided that was what I wanted to do. When I set out for California, I went with this dream in my heart: to get my education, become a model, and never return to Mississippi.

Little did I know that God had something completely different in mind for me.

Chapter Three
A Change Of Plans: Meeting and marrying Dolphus Weary

Like many young, black and poor Mississippians growing up in the 1950s and '60s, I picked my share of cotton. It would be hard to overstate how unpleasant picking cotton is. For one thing, the harvest takes place during late August and early September—a time of year when the heat and humidity conspire to make any movement, no matter how slight, a sweat-inducing activity.

On these hottest of days, we arrived at the fields around sunrise, picked up eight-foot sacks, and began the arduous task of trudging between the rows, backs bent and aching, pulling cotton from the bolls and stuffing it into the sacks. When your sack became so heavy you couldn't drag it any more, you waited for the owner of the field to come by in his truck, weigh what you had picked so far, and record the amount in his book. I weighed less than 100 pounds when I started picking cotton; sometimes the sack I'd been pulling came in at 30 pounds.

Even working from sunup to sundown, I hardly ever managed to pick more than 100 pounds in a day. Since the going rate was somewhere around $2 per 100 pounds (a little less for first pickings when the cotton was heavier, a little more for later pickings), my hourly wage came out to be approximately 15¢.

As difficult and minimally rewarding as the work was, I do have the cotton fields of Mississippi to thank for one thing: They are where I met the man who would eventually become my husband.

Not that it was love at first sight, mind you. Our initial meeting was pretty mundane, to tell the truth. Some of my siblings and I happened to be picking cotton in the same field as Dolphus and some of his brothers and sisters, and we all talked casually over the course of the day. As a result of that encounter, Dolphus actually became interested in my sister, Earlene. She didn't return his affections, and for a while after that, the only connection between our two families was that Dolphus rode to and from his school, Harper High, on the bus my father drove.

It wasn't until the summer of 1968, when I participated in the Sunday School Institute hosted by Voice of Calvary, that Dolphus and I really got to know each other. As you may recall, Dolphus and my friend, Carolyn, were both on staff with VOC that summer, and I ended up volunteering with the ministry quite a bit.

Dolphus, Carolyn and I spent a lot of time together that summer, having long conversations about all sorts of things. We all helped lead Vacation Bible Schools in the community, so we often planned lessons together, and we also discussed our ideas about ministry and church more generally. We were concerned about the fact that so many churches seemed to emphasize church membership rather than salvation through faith in Christ. Other conversations focused on the racial climate in the state, and on our hopes and dreams for the future.

As was probably true for many young people at that time, our thoughts about the future were filled with contradictions and extremes of emotion. On one hand, we all clung to our fantasies of leaving, being wildly successful, and never coming back. On the other hand, we were investing tremendous amounts of time and energy, and putting our very lives at risk, marching with Rev. Perkins and otherwise joining in local activism and outreach. We were simultaneously hopeful that things would change and terrified that something bad would happen to us before they did. To paraphrase one of Mrs. Perkins's favorite Bible club songs, we were trying to find our way through the wilderness, trusting that the Lord would lead us, but not able to see the road ahead very clearly.

Dolphus, already an up-and-coming leader in the community, made special efforts to include me in projects or tasks he was involved in. Later, I would find out that he was already interested in me during this season, but at the time I couldn't see that, either.

Toward the end of the summer, several young adults, along with about 25 youth, went to Cedine Bible Camp in Spring City, Tennessee. Camp Cedine was a lovely place in a wooded area—a welcome change of scenery for African-American youth, many of whom had very few opportunities to venture outside their home communities. I had certainly never been to camp before, though not for want of trying. Camp Pioneer in Jackson offered scholarships to youth who memorized a certain number of Bible verses over the course of a year. I had memorized the verses each year for several years, but because there were still incidental costs involved (including providing your own transportation to and from camp), I was never able to attend.

I remember arriving at Camp Cedine that first time: On the right were some swings, the dining area, tetherball poles and basketball goals; to the left were the girls' cabins, an arts and crafts building, and the place where boats and equipment were stored. A little farther in that direction, there was a beautiful lake, and lakeside cabins for the staff members.

Camp was great fun. I tried archery for the first time in my life and discovered I was pretty good at it. We did all sorts of arts and crafts projects, and I decided I was finally going to learn how to swim. On my first attempt, I nearly drowned. I jumped right in, went under the water, and then couldn't get myself back above the surface. I had to be rescued by one of the camp counselors. That was a terrifying experience, naturally, but I was determined to learn, so I tried again the next day. That time, I was considerably more cautious, and things went a lot more smoothly.

At daily chapel services, we had the privilege of hearing some truly beautiful singing. I especially remember a group of African-American women with lovely voices who worshipped the Lord through a rendition of Psalm 61.

In between scheduled activities, Dolphus and I went on long walks together, talking and talking, and even though we were clearly drawn to each other, I still didn't expect that we would start dating. What was foremost on my mind was education, so one of the recurring conversations we had that was most interesting to me was the one about my attending Los Angeles Baptist College.

Many years later, on Dolphus's 60th birthday, I would write him a letter, acknowledging that this summer was when I secretly fell in love with him. At the time, though, between not knowing how he felt about me and being focused on my education, I didn't allow myself to hope for, or even think much about, more than the good friendship we were developing.

At LABC, the group from Mississippi spent a lot of time together—traveling with the basketball team, going into L.A. to visit other friends from our home state, going to Disneyland (friends in Santa Ana gave us tickets), and going into town for pizza or to eat at Mr. Steak. Dolphus and Jimmie were the comedians of our group. They were funny and loud, and they kept us laughing (and nearby patrons in the restaurants we visited staring). I tended to stay quiet when we were all out together, but when it was just Dolphus and me, I was more talkative, maybe because he seemed genuinely interested in the things I had to say.

Each semester, the college held a banquet for the students. These dinners would be held at fancy off-campus venues, with gorgeous decorations, and everybody dressed up in their best "after five" clothes. The first fall I was at LABC, Dolphus attended the banquet with Carolyn, and I went with another young man from our group. To be completely honest, I would have preferred to go with Dolphus, just as friends, but since he and Carolyn were already making plans to attend the banquet together, that wasn't really an option.

I had thought Dolphus and Carolyn might end up becoming a couple after the banquet, but they didn't. Around this same time, Mrs. Perkins, a persistent matchmaker with a decent success rate (I'd estimate around 40 percent), decided to set Carolyn up with a young man from Mendenhall named Artis Fletcher. Artis had gone off to Washington, D.C., where he attended Washington Bible College, then founded and pastored a church in Aberdeen, Maryland. Artis and Carolyn spent time together during the summers, when they both returned to Mendenhall to visit their families, and they eventually married. Artis finished his schooling at LABC, and he has now served for many years as the beloved pastor of Mendenhall Bible Church.

Spring rolled around, and Dolphus invited me to attend the next banquet as his date. The spring banquet was even more formal than the fall event, and everyone went all out to prepare for it. I hadn't brought any formal clothes to school with me, so I wrote my mother and asked her to mail me the dress I'd worn when I was crowned homecoming queen in high school.

My new roommate (my first roommate had gotten married) was a few years older than I was, and she was a licensed beautician. She really wanted to do my hair for the banquet, and I accepted her offer. I straightened it myself, then let her go to work. It wasn't long before she discovered how different "black hair" is from "white hair." My hair did not behave the way she expected it to. Fortunately, she had plenty of hairspray handy, so she was able to coax my hair into a "do" that lasted through the banquet.

I was so exhausted from class and work that I actually fell asleep in the car on the rides to and from the banquet (which was held on a beautifully decorated boat-turned-restaurant), but Dolphus didn't seem to take that personally, and we had a great time at the dinner. Shortly after that, Dolphus and I became an item. This was a great source of relief to the school administration, who were concerned by the fact that several white girls had crushes on Dolphus, who was, after all, a handsome and charismatic basketball star. Interracial dating was taboo at LABC—if there were any interracial couples on campus, they kept their secrets well, because I never knew of any.

Neither of us having much money, and Dolphus, like my father and grandfather, being so tight with a dollar he could put it out of circulation, our dating life was fairly low-key.

"Hey, let's go get something to drink at Thrifty," Dolphus might say when he came over. So we'd walk into town, or take the VW bug that Dolphus and Jimmie shared, buy a Mother's Pride two-liter bottle of soda and some ice, and sit and drink it. Or we'd go down to the snack shop at the gym for licorice. On the rare occasions when we went out to dinner, it was to Mr. Steak or Denny's—nothing fancy.

Soon after we began dating, I discovered one of the many ways that Dolphus and I are very different from each other. Dolphus is one of those "touchy-feely" people, and he always wanted to hug me, or hold my hand, even in public. I was extremely uncomfortable with that—hugging was simply not something we did in my family—until I spent time with *his* family and saw that they were all just like him. Once I realized where he was coming from, his behavior seemed less like he was trying to put the moves on me, and more like he was just being affectionate.

Though hugging remains a little awkward for me, I eventually got used to and even came to appreciate the value of this gesture. Over time, I've introduced hugging into my relationships with my siblings, some of whom appreciate it, others of whom merely tolerate it. Sometimes, I let those family members off the hook and revert to shaking hands when I see them.

Even after Dolphus and I had been dating for almost a year, marriage remained the last thing on my mind. I had come to school to get an education and work my plan—to become a fashion model, or, failing that, begin a teaching career. Dolphus, as has often been the case, was a step or two (or more) ahead of me, making payments on the ring he'd picked out and planning how he would propose. (Once I found out about all that, I realized his frugality during our dating months hadn't been stinginess; he'd just been budgeting carefully so he could afford the ring and save toward marriage!)

Believe it or not, I actually broke up with Dolphus not long before he asked me to marry him. It wasn't that he'd done anything wrong—in fact, neither of us can remember any more the specific reason I gave for my decision—and I really did like him a lot, but I broke it off anyway. My main concerns, I think, were that our relationship was distracting me from my studies, and it seemed to be becoming more serious than I was sure I was ready for it to be. We were only apart for a few weeks, but I remember that time being really difficult. Dolphus and I tried to avoid each other, but that's hard on a small campus, especially when you have all of the same friends.

Then came a Sadie Hawkins-style event, on the evening of one of the home basketball games. I went to the game, as I always did, and afterwards I saw Dolphus just sort of standing around. So I asked him out, even though I had to tell him up front that I didn't have enough money to pay for our meal, so he would have to chip in. And, since he had a vehicle and I didn't, he would have to drive. Dolphus didn't object to either of those conditions. We went to Paul's Pizzeria that night, and after that we were back together, as everyone who knew us had assumed we would be.

As my 20th birthday approached, Dolphus told me he wanted to take me to dinner in Santa Monica, and that I should dress up for the occasion. On the morning of my birthday, Dolphus gave me a card, flowers and a box of candy. I was surprised by the extravagance, but still didn't guess what was coming. That evening, a Chinese student who lived down the hall from me saw me in my fancy blue dress and asked where I was going. When I told her, she offered to lend me her white fur jacket to complete the outfit.

We drove the forty-five minutes or so to Santa Monica and arrived at a beautiful seaside restaurant that Dolphus had chosen on the recommendation of one of his professors. They seated us at a table overlooking the ocean; waves lapped against the windows as we looked at the menu, and Dolphus told me to order anything I wanted. I actually thought he might be ill—he didn't look well, and he certainly wasn't acting like himself.

After dinner, Dolphus made a little speech (during which I kept thinking, "Where is he going with this?"), pulled out a ring box, took my hand, and asked if I would marry him.

"We need to pray," I said, caught completely off guard. That probably wasn't what he was expecting to hear, but we did pray.

Dolphus had an awful lot going for him, as a potential life partner. I knew he loved the Lord, and he clearly had a compassionate heart. He was kind, thoughtful, smart and funny, and he seemed very stable. Like he would be a good family man. And he was a good listener. He always made me feel like I had something to offer, like I was special. He was also quite handsome. In short, he was very nearly everything I could possibly want in a husband.

Still, I wasn't positive I should say yes to his proposal.

If I'm honest, there were two things that caused my hesitation. The first was my plan to pursue a career, and the fact that I still hadn't been thinking about marriage, even though we had resumed our dating relationship. The second is that, for a long time, I had hoped to marry someone who had money and could give me some of the things I had never had. Now here was Dolphus, whose family was just as poor as mine, asking me to marry him. I wasn't sure I could agree to the kind of life we would almost certainly have together.

But as we prayed, I sensed God saying, "Rosie, this is who I have for you."

So, figuring I could still change my mind later if I realized I'd made a mistake, I opened my eyes and said yes. I hadn't really had any peace about it until that moment, but when I accepted Dolphus's proposal, God's peace came over me, and I felt certain that I had made the right decision. This was a man I could build a life with. Maybe we would make some money together, maybe we wouldn't, but suddenly that mattered less than it had even a few minutes earlier.

When I arrived back at the dorm, around midnight, I ran into another student from Mississippi, Mary Norwood, in the bathroom. She gave my outfit a once-over. "You look so nice…" she started to compliment me. Then she saw the ring. Without another word to me, Mary—who was always a little bit crazy in a fun way—ran into the hallway, screaming to the top of her voice, "Rosie's engaged, Rosie's engaged!"

I didn't want to be any part of the ruckus, so I ran to my room and closed the door. Before long, the RAs came knocking. "People are trying to sleep," they said.

"I didn't say anything," I told them, truthfully.

By the next morning at breakfast, the whole school knew—professors, everybody.

My parents had recently gotten their first telephone, so I called them from the pay phone in the dorm to share the news with them. Their response was much more subdued than Mary's. "That's good," they said when I told them we were planning to get married. They hadn't been expecting the news, but they had always liked Dolphus and didn't have any objection to our engagement.

Almost immediately, I started thinking—and worrying—about how I was going to pay for a wedding. My parents wouldn't be able to help much. I started saving toward it, but the only job I had at that point was a part-time work study position in the school library. I held onto the peace God had given me at the restaurant—if this was really His will, He would work it out.

The day after we got engaged, Dolphus received news that put a slight wrinkle in our plans—he learned that he would be traveling to Asia with Overseas Crusades' Ventures for Victory basketball outreach program. Dolphus had proposed on my birthday (February 26), and he'd hoped we could get married on his birthday (August 7), but because of his travel plans, we pushed the date back to August 15.

Before the spring semester ended, we had one two-hour counseling session with a professor on campus. That was the extent of the pre-marital counseling we would receive, and I remember very little of what he told us. Something about what a serious commitment we were making, and how we would need to work at it—it wouldn't always be easy, but we shouldn't run away. I think he also gave us a book to read. Other than that, we were pretty much on our own as far as preparing for marriage, and with Dolphus leaving the country in May and not returning until the end of June, I would be very much on my own as far as many of the wedding preparations were concerned.

I returned to Mississippi at the beginning of the summer and went straight to the library, where I checked out a book about weddings. The book was helpful, but many of its recommendations would require serious money to implement, so I had to modify the ideas I wanted to use to fit my budget. As I began to make my plans, I discovered that I wasn't quite as on my own as I'd thought. My sister Earlene, who had gotten married a couple of years before, agreed to lend me her dress: a simple but beautiful white gown with a long train and a mesh veil.

When I decided to buy material and have the bridesmaids' dresses made, figuring that would be cheaper than buying dresses, a Voice of Calvary volunteer, Chris Erb, offered to do the sewing for free as her wedding gift. Mrs. Perkins agreed to make the wedding cake, and a number of other ladies from the community and VOC said they would bring food for the reception.

I visited a little flower shop, somewhere between the towns of Plain and Florence, and the woman who owned it said she had never done an African-American wedding. Far from being reluctant to venture into this new territory, she was excited about the opportunity and gave us a really good deal on the flowers. One of Dolphus's professors from Piney Woods, Mr. Phifer, offered to take photos for us as a wedding gift. My sister Esta accompanied and advised me as I made all these arrangements and preparations.

And throughout this time, Dolphus and I wrote each other letters. I wrote to him every day, sending him Scripture verses to read and keeping him updated about my progress planning our wedding. He was incredibly busy, so he couldn't write as often, but he would send me a letter whenever he could. Among other things, we discussed the question of starting a family, and we agreed that we wouldn't have children right away, since we were both still in school (I would be a junior, and Dolphus was now a student at the seminary affiliated with our college).

Along with my other preparations, I spent the summer trying to gain a Biblical perspective on being a wife, but without counseling or instruction, what I came up with was vague at best. I had a sense that I was supposed to be submissive to my husband, love him, and make sure his needs were met, but I didn't know exactly what that looked like. I knew I was supposed to take care of our home—and since I was not marrying a man with the means to hire someone to help around the house, that meant I would be doing the household-related stuff myself. That was about all I knew.

Not surprisingly, I suffered a lot of anxiety and "cold feet" that summer. I asked myself over and over again if I knew how to be a good wife. Was I really ready for this? And over and over again, I thought back to the peace God had given me about saying yes.

Dolphus returned from his overseas travels at the end of June, and we spent the next six weeks finishing the wedding preparations—getting the men fitted for their tuxes, making honeymoon plans, finalizing details with the florist, and so on. Every day, there was something we needed to do.

Between wedding-related errands, Dolphus gave me a series of gifts he'd brought back for me from Asia. Dolphus loves surprises, so he didn't tell me at first that there would be more than one gift. The first day, he just said, "This is something I picked up for you," and gave me three necklaces made from colorful handmade beads. Then each day, for seven days, he presented me with another beautiful gift he'd acquired as he traveled: a silk slip, a kimono, a silk umbrella, a pair of sunglasses, a jewelry box, an ivory necklace, and a jade ring. The whole thing was very romantic, and I was deeply touched that, with all the other demands on his time and attention, Dolphus had gone out of his way to find something special for me from each place the team visited. To this day, I have kept all of those gifts (as well as all of the letters Dolphus sent me from abroad). The jewelry box was damaged recently, when our house was broken into and the thieves dropped it on the ground while the police were chasing them, but I treasure it still and intend to have it repaired.

At the last minute, we discovered that we needed to find a new minister to officiate our ceremony. Rev. Perkins had originally agreed to do it, even though he was still recovering from the severe beating he had suffered at the hands of white highway patrol officers earlier that year. Over the summer, though, his doctors decided he needed additional surgery, and the operation was scheduled for the same week as our wedding. Dolphus's brother-in-law, Rev. Robert Clayton, came to our rescue, agreeing to marry us even though he had two other weddings scheduled for the same day. He married one couple very early that morning (early enough that the bride and groom could still report to work on time), us at 3:00 in the afternoon, and a third couple at 5:00 that evening.

Our wedding was held at my home church, New Zion Baptist in Pinola. When I arrived at the church to get dressed, the place was deserted. It was fairly rare for African Americans in our community to have church weddings, and suddenly I was struck by the fear that no one was coming. I finished my preparations, and I was still afraid the church would be empty. So Esta went to check the parking lot and soon returned, smiling. "Relax," she told me. "There are cars everywhere."

Despite all my worries, the wedding itself turned out beautifully. Carolyn, Dolphus's sister Pat, my sisters Esta and Eula, and my friend Catherine Norwood were my bridesmaids. My sister, Sandra, was our flower girl, and our ring-bearer was Jackie Ray McIntosh. Our junior bridesmaid and groomsman were my niece, Phyllis, and a boy from VOC's youth program, Rodney Skiffer. Just a kid at the time, today Rodney is retired from a career with the State of Mississippi, and his wife has served as both principal of Genesis One Christian School and as the interim president of The Mendenhall Ministries, the organization that grew out of the ministry that brought us all together in the first place. Standing with Dolphus at the front of the church were his brother Melvin, my brother W.C., and friends Harold Johnson, Artis Fletcher and Jimmie Walker.

As my father walked me down the aisle, I was nervous, I was excited, and I had no idea what lay ahead of me. I was pretty sure about a couple of things. I knew God was in it, and I knew that life with Dolphus would be an adventure, one way or another.

Punctuality is important to both Dolphus and me, so our wedding actually started very close to on-time, which probably surprised many of the people in attendance. We had also decided to keep the ceremony short and sweet. Rev. Clayton said a few words, we exchanged our vows and rings, and we had music by Don London, as well as a beautiful rendition of the Lord's Prayer by Catherine Norwood.

After the ceremony, we went up to Voice of Calvary for the reception. Mrs. Perkins had made a lovely two-tiered wedding cake for us. Elgia Clayton (Dolphus's sister and Rev. Clayton's wife), Alzean Skiffer (Rodney's mother), Nancy Hamilton, and a number of other ladies from the community had done a wonderful job with the reception. As eager as Dolphus and I had both been to leave Mississippi behind us, we couldn't deny that there was good food back home!

We spent our wedding night in Jackson, then drove up to Mound Bayou the next morning to see Rev. Perkins in the hospital. After visiting with him, we set off for Florida, planning to spend our honeymoon in Miami. There was no such thing as Mapquest back then, and we soon realized we had misjudged how long the drive was going to take. We made it as far as Tampa and decided, if we didn't want to spend our *whole* honeymoon in the car, we should stop there and stay for a couple of days.

We returned to Mendenhall, each of us staying with our own parents for the two or three days we had to pack up and prepare for school, and then it was time to get back to Los Angeles. Dolphus was working as a resident advisor (RA) now, and the school had called to tell us we would be able to live in one of the two RA apartments on campus, so that was a blessing. But, the apartment was unfurnished, and we didn't have any furniture, so we were anxious about that as we headed west once more.

It turns out we didn't have to worry. When we got to campus and opened our apartment door, we discovered rooms full of furniture and appliances. Students and faculty had given or lent us nearly everything we needed.

I worked in the campus library again that year, and in addition to his RA job and seminary studies, Dolphus worked nights at the Thrifty Mart, ran the college's intramural sports program, and coached the freshman basketball team. I also had Christian service assignments through school (I taught Sunday School classes in Compton and volunteered at JOY (Jesus, Others and You) clubs, as well). During the holiday season, I added a part-time job at a JC Penney in the San Fernando Valley to my already full schedule.

Dolphus and I probably saw each other less that first year of marriage than we had while we were dating, and if we hadn't been living together, we might not have seen each other at all.

Our first Christmas as a married couple was challenging. Between the cost of traveling and our work commitments, Dolphus didn't think we should make the trip to Mississippi for the holiday. While I understood his reasoning, it was only my second time not being home at Christmas, and I missed my family terribly.

A kind couple from the seminary, the Thornburgs, let us use their apartment for the holiday, so we could at least get off campus. I prepared to cook my first Christmas dinner on my own—turkey, dressing, the works. The turkey (I didn't attempt a whole one, just boiled some parts) turned out fine. The cornbread dressing was another story. I had watched Mama make it so many times, I just knew I could do it right, but I forgot how much broth was needed. I put in way too much cornbread and ended up with a horrible, gummy mess. I threw it away, in tears, while Dolphus graciously tried to comfort me. "It's okay, Rosie, it's not a big deal," he said.

But to me, it was a big deal. Whatever else I did or didn't know about being a good wife, I felt certain that I ought to be able to prepare a decent Christmas dinner for my husband. So I resolved that I would really learn how to cook, and I began asking my mother for specific instructions about how she made all the dishes I'd watched her prepare while I was growing up.

Although I had longed to be in Mississippi for Christmas, we had a different homecoming ahead of us that had been much harder to think about when Dolphus first proposed it. During his overseas basketball trip the summer before, Dolphus had been the only black player on his team, and children in Hong Kong, the Philippines and Taiwan had been fascinated by this high-jumping, dark-skinned young man. The team kept busy, often playing as many as three games a day, with team members sharing their testimonies during halftime. After each game, groups of kids would surround Dolphus, touching his skin and then checking their hands to see if he was covered in paint that would rub off on them.

His coach, seeing how quickly Dolphus established a good rapport with local young people, asked him if he would consider doing full-time missions work in Asia after he finished school.

"Anywhere but Mississippi," Dolphus had replied, in a light-hearted but not really joking way. He'd had even less intention than I did of ever going back.

After that conversation, as Dolphus spent time in prayer, he sensed the Holy Spirit asking him, "Are you going to a mission field or are you running away from a mission field?" He wrestled with this question for weeks before acknowledging that yes, he had been running away. And more importantly, that he was willing to go back, if that was really what God wanted.

Dolphus knew this was something he and I should talk about *before* we got married, so as soon as he returned from his trip, he shared with me how God was leading him. *What would I think about returning to Mississippi to participate in the work John and Vera Mae Perkins and others were doing there?* he wanted to know. I was stunned, of course, to find out that Dolphus was even thinking about going back, and I didn't have any desire to go back, but because we had prayed before I accepted his marriage proposal, I knew God wouldn't separate us.

And I did want to be in God's will, after all.

But I also wanted to be a fashion model, possibly a teacher, and definitely not poor—and the opportunities to pursue those goals seemed so much greater in California.

Finally, I told Dolphus, "I don't sense God's calling to Mississippi, but if you do, I'm willing to trust that, and I'll go with you."

In the end, it probably wasn't as hard a decision for me to make as it had been for Dolphus. It would be good to be close to my family again, and I could still finish my education and prepare for a teaching career there. Even so, to let go of my modeling dream and step back into the still very real shadows of a racially divided and impoverished Mississippi—these were not easy things to do.

Chapter Four
From Segregation To Reconciliation: Mississippi's changing race relations

As with so many Mississippi memories, one thing I recall from that night in June 1968 is how hot it was. Even at three in the morning, in the non-air conditioned upstairs room at John and Vera Mae Perkins's house where Carolyn and I were staying, the heat was stifling.

I couldn't sleep—partly because of the temperature and partly because I felt bad about an interaction I'd had with Mrs. Perkins that morning. Carolyn and I had recently graduated from high school, and Carolyn had arranged to stay at the Perkins family's home that summer, so she didn't have to commute from Harrisville to Mendenhall every day to work at Voice of Calvary. More recently, she'd had the idea that I should stay there, too, since I was volunteering with the ministry. Carolyn had cleared her plan with Rev. Perkins, but apparently nobody told Mrs. Perkins to expect an additional houseguest.

The first morning I was there, I was in the kitchen making breakfast for everyone when Mrs. Perkins walked in. I doubt Vera Mae Perkins has ever beaten around a bush in her life. "Who are you, and why are you here?" she demanded of me, without preamble, that morning. I knew Mrs. Perkins, of course, from the school chapel services and weekly VOC Bible studies, but to her I had just been one more face in the crowd. Now, here I was in her home, uninvited as far as she was concerned. Technically, I don't think the mix-up was my fault, but still, I felt terrible.

Since I couldn't get to sleep, I sat up late into the night, reading. After a while, I became aware of a vehicle driving slowly by the house. I crept to the window and looked out. As the car passed under an outdoor light Rev. Perkins had installed to illuminate the otherwise dark street, I saw that it was filled with white men. There was no way this could be good. I waited, and sure enough, the car drove around the block and passed the house again.

Quietly, I went downstairs and awakened Rev. and Mrs. Perkins. "There's a carload of white folks keep driving by the house," I whispered. Rev. Perkins watched as they drove past again, real slow. Then he went and got his gun. That scared me nearly to death.

The next time the car drove by, Rev. Perkins shot over the men's heads. They immediately pulled onto the co-op property across the street, turned the car around, and peeled out of there in a hurry. I've never seen someone turn a car around that fast! The sound of the shot wakened the rest of the household—the Perkins kids, Carolyn, and a white volunteer who was also staying there that summer. We huddled together as Rev. Perkins called the police and told them exactly what had happened. I'm not sure what kind of response he expected, but he got no sympathy from the officer who answered the phone.

"You had no business shooting," the policeman said, angrily. Then he added a vague threat. "If you shoot that gun again…" No officers came out to take a statement or investigate the incident, and they certainly didn't offer any protection.

They never had. That's why, earlier on, members of the community had spent many nights sitting in a ditch outside the Perkins house, keeping watch for potential attackers. The watches had stopped, as it had seemed like things were quieting down. The events of this night alerted us that the danger was not yet past.

I don't know what those men had planned—maybe they were only trying to intimidate us, maybe they would have taken all of our lives, maybe something in between. I never will know what might have happened that night, but I do know that I'm grateful God kept me awake. As unpleasant as the heat and my feelings of guilt may have been, they certainly served a useful purpose on that occasion.

During the dog days of earlier Mississippi summers, I'd had other opportunities to observe racial disparities and injustice up close, while I was picking cotton in fields owned by white families. I'd look around the back of the truck, where we workers were stuffed like cattle, being driven out to the part of the field where we'd be picking that day, and I'd notice that there were no white faces there. It wasn't that the owner of the field didn't have any kids our ages, it was that the white kids were all in school, while the black kids were providing low-cost labor and falling further and further behind in our educations.

One day, when I was about 13, a white girl came to the field where we were working, I guess to visit the field owner's son, who was driving the truck that day. Before I knew what was happening, the son punched one of the black male workers in the stomach so hard he fell to the ground. The reason? According to the son, the worker had said something to the white girl. I hadn't heard him say anything, and he would have been crazy to actually do anything to a white woman in front of a white man. I don't know, maybe he said hello or asked her a question or something. Whatever he had or hadn't done, this incident certainly helped open my eyes to the dynamics of race and power. That white boy knew he wouldn't be punished for the violence he inflicted, and the black boy was lucky nothing worse happened to him. Just a few years earlier, Emmett Till had been brutally murdered for allegedly whistling at a white girl.

About this same time, I started hearing about the Ku Klux Klan reviving its presence in our area. We'd all been told horror stories about the lynchings that had happened in previous decades. Now we started hearing new rumors about people getting beaten or disappearing. John Perkins and others were receiving threats, churches were being burned, and the Klan's sheet-clad members would march down streets in broad daylight. Supposedly, some of these Klansmen were also Deacons in their churches. We didn't have a television, but people who did would tell us about things they saw on the evening news. Meanwhile, our parents gave us strict instructions about what we could and couldn't do as they tried desperately to keep their children safe.

Mama was too scared for Daddy to ever really get involved in the Civil Rights Movement. He did go to some of the meetings, but he never marched. My mother's fears were not without basis. Our church, New Zion, opened its doors to meetings for a while, but then one Sunday we arrived for service and saw where someone had tried to light a fire. Eventually, the church did burn down, and we had to rebuild. I don't know if it was arson or not—we always assumed it was, but no one was ever caught or punished for setting the fire.

On an individual level, my father did take a stand against racial discrimination. Daddy had started driving a school bus when I was in the sixth or seventh grade. He took the job initially because he needed the additional income, but he loved the kids and ended up driving for many years, until after I'd gone off to college. Once, though, when the white county Superintendent made a racial slur, Daddy quit driving and refused to go back, even when the Superintendent sent a friend of my father's—a well respected African-American pastor—to try to convince him to start driving again. It was about two years before Daddy agreed to return to work for the school system.

Because we were isolated from the rest of the world in so many ways, I don't remember knowing very much about what was happening nationally while I was growing up. I was only four when the Brown v. Board of Education verdict was handed down, so even though that decision eventually affected all of us, I don't remember it as a landmark event of my childhood. I do recall hearing that the new high school building we got at New Hymn had something to do with some sort of government action—something about "separate but equal." I was 10 when Ruby Bridges integrated an all-white elementary school in New Orleans, and I do remember listening to radio reports about the federal marshals who escorted her as she braved that hostile environment.

My parents voted for the first time in 1964, even though the Voting Rights Act wasn't passed until 1965, and federal voting registrars didn't arrive in our state until 1966. John Perkins and the folks at VOC, along with others in the community, had been working hard to register Blacks to vote, even though doing so put their lives in danger and the ministry's funding at risk. I'm so proud of my parents for being brave enough to go to the polls that day. I know my mother, especially, must have been scared.

My uncle, Isaac "Ike" Black, voted in the '64 election, as well. If Uncle Ike felt any fear about the possible consequences of registering and voting, he sure didn't show it. Like Daddy, he was a school bus driver, and I was on his route. I remember him telling all of us, as we boarded his bus, how proud he was to have voted for Lyndon Johnson. "We went and messed up ol' Goldwater today," he said gleefully.

Of course, I also remember vividly the day Lyndon Johnson had first assumed the office of President—the day John F. Kennedy was assassinated. I was at school, and some seniors came running down the hall, crying. I didn't know what was going on. Then the Principal's wife ran into the hall, saying, "They shot our man, they shot our man." Finally, I understood that President Kennedy had been killed. We all sat in our classrooms, crying, for a long time.

What a terribly bleak day that was. We didn't just mourn the murder of a human being, although of course we did grieve for President Kennedy and his family. Mixed in with our sadness was fear for our own futures. We had finally had a President who cared about us and our plight, and now he was gone. We kept asking each other the same questions: *What are we going to do? Who's going to speak for us now?*

The mood on the school bus going home that day was somber, and I remember my uncle then, too. He'd been so sad. "They got our man," he said as I stepped onto his bus.

A few years later, during my senior year, it was the same scene all over again, when Dr. Martin Luther King Jr. was killed. In a way, this was even more devastating, because Dr. King was a black man who'd had the courage to confront discrimination head-on. He preached (and practiced) nonviolence, but at the same time he showed us how we could stand up for ourselves and taught us that we could change the world around us. It was so bad in Mississippi, and we were always so scared—we saw Dr. King as a savior of sorts.

I remember watching the funeral procession on television and seeing the pain on Mrs. King's face. And again we asked each other, and ourselves: *What's going to happen now? Who's going to stand up and take his place?*

Whether or not we realized it at the time, at least part of the answer to that second question was: *We are.* While Dr. King's death was a horrible blow, it also made many of us even more determined to do what we could to carry on his dream by working for justice in our own communities.

In December of 1969, just after Dolphus, Carolyn and I returned from college for our Christmas break, a young man from Mendenhall was arrested for arguing with a white store owner. Fearing for the young man's safety in jail, Rev. Perkins, Carolyn, a few other adults, and a number of children, some as young as five, went up to the station to talk to the police. Before long, the whole group was locked up, including the kids. People from the community soon heard about what had happened and began gathering outside the jailhouse.

Through the jail cell window, Rev. Perkins addressed the crowd and proposed action that would hit the white community where it would hurt: in their pocketbooks at Christmas-time. The theory was that if white businesspeople lost enough money, they would put pressure on city officials to address the concerns of the black community and end the boycott.

The children were released that night, the rest of the group the next day. By the time they got out, Vera Mae Perkins, Nathan Rubin, Jesse Newsome, Mitchell Hayes and other local leaders were already hard at work, getting the boycott underway. They provided transport to nearby Magee so people could do their holiday shopping there and organized marches through downtown Mendenhall.

On one of these marches, I walked alongside Vera Mae Perkins. Even though we had a permit to march, one car sped down the street where we were walking. It came so close to me, I could feel the burn on my leg, and I realized if it had come just a couple of feet closer, it would have run us both over.

Mrs. Perkins and I also passed a store where two merchants were sitting together, watching us go by. One of them had always been friendly when we shopped at his store, but now pure venom came out of his mouth. The two men pointed at us and called out racial slurs.

"Rosie, do you believe this?" Mrs. Perkins asked me, shocked.

"No, I don't," I said. We continued to march, hand in hand, holding onto each other as if for dear life.

Even after the boycott ended, it would be a long, long time before I would return to this man's store. Rev. Perkins told me once that this merchant said to him, "The only thing Blacks can do for me is clean my house, cook my food and take care of my children." I have to say, I have never understood this rationale. Why would a person put his own health and the well-being of his children in the hands of someone he didn't respect or trust? I suppose this is just one of many ways that racism defies logic, but it has always puzzled me.

Years after the boycott, I learned that this man had begun hiring African Americans to work in his store. At that point, I finally felt all right about patronizing his business again.

Ultimately, the boycott was successful. The merchants realized they would really suffer if we didn't buy from them, and the business and civic leaders became a little more willing to listen to our concerns. It was a small victory, but an important one for a group of people who had been powerless and voiceless for so long.

But before that victory, there was more hardship to be endured. When our group returned to California after the holidays, the Mendenhall boycott was still going on. One Saturday in February 1970, John Perkins was arrested again, along with a couple of neighbors from Mendenhall, a white VOC volunteer, and a bunch of Tougaloo College students. Most, if not all, of those arrested were beaten by highway patrol officers while in custody. Rev. Perkins took the worst of it. He almost died from the torture they inflicted on him.

Mrs. Perkins called us in California to tell us what was happening. She asked us to get as many students together as we could to pray for her husband and the others. We felt helpless, being so far away. No one could afford the airfare to get back to Mississippi, and we really couldn't have done anything if we were there, anyway. So we did what Mrs. Perkins asked us to do. We got a group of students—black and white—together, and we prayed. One blessing to come out of this terrible event is that it became a turning point for some of the white students on our campus. Hearing what had happened to Rev. Perkins convinced them that the injustices and dangers we'd been talking about were real. We weren't making things up.

As we prayed for Rev. Perkins from California, and as we waited impatiently for news of his condition, many thoughts and emotions swirled through my head and heart. I was outraged, of course, that someone I knew and cared about had been treated so cruelly and unjustly. And not just someone I knew, but a godly man. A man who, like Dr. King, preached nonviolence. Rev. Perkins never encouraged the people he led to resort to violence. He didn't try to incite riots or rile folks up. He just saw that his people were suffering and tried to find ways for folks to work together and treat each other with dignity. Even when people refused to do right by us, he said we should deal with them through their pocketbooks—never by inflicting physical harm on them.

So I was angry that a group of people—and not just any people, but people who were supposed to "serve and protect"—had chosen to inflict such terrible harm on him.

I was also afraid—afraid for Rev. Perkins's life, afraid for Mrs. Perkins and the children if he didn't survive, and afraid more people I loved would be hurt. Even though we'd always known that participating in the Movement put us in danger, this tragedy brought that truth home to us in a new way.

At the same time, I felt pity for the people who had committed these savage, senseless acts because of their hatred. I felt sorry for them because they had lowered themselves to such base standards. I also pitied them because they'd degraded themselves for nothing, in the sense that they were ultimately unsuccessful in what they were trying to accomplish. I'm sure they thought if they caused enough fear, we would stop the work we were doing. Instead, Rev. Perkins's beating, like Dr. King's and President Kennedy's assassinations, motivated us to work harder, to do more. Yes, we were afraid, but we didn't give up. I don't remember even entertaining the possibility. For the first time in my life, I was standing up for something that was much bigger than I was, and I wasn't about to sit back down.

My ongoing involvement in civil rights activities was a source of mixed emotions for my parents. Daddy was proud of me for doing what I believed was right—for doing what I'm pretty sure he would have done if Mama had let him. But I know he worried about me. And Mama remained very fearful about the whole thing. She prayed all the time, begged me to be careful, and probably would have preferred that I didn't get involved. But, as with my decision to go out of state for college, she knew that I was going to do what I had made up my mind to do, so she never really tried to stop me.

In addition to John and Vera Mae Perkins, who are probably the best-known leaders of the civil rights efforts in Simpson County, I had the privilege of knowing and working alongside a number of other brave men and women who labored tirelessly for the Movement.

Mr. and Mrs. Nathan Rubin, and their grown daughter Myrtis, were heavily involved in the voter registration drives. Mr. Rubin wasn't afraid of anything, and he would drive way out into the boonies to help people get registered. Farmers by trade, the Rubins were very community oriented, and they loved young people, so they would informally adopt many of the white youth who came down to help. Mrs. Rubin never hesitated to open her home and provide food for the volunteers who participated in the Movement in our community. Before school desegregation was enforced in Mississippi, the Rubins sent their younger daughter, Kathy, to the white school in Mendenhall. The two oldest Perkins children, Spencer and Joanie, went there as well. All three had a terrible time of it, and Spencer and Joanie returned to the black school after two years. Kathy stayed through to graduation.

Mr. Rubin died a few years ago, and one of my regrets in life is that we didn't do more to honor him and the important work he did. If I had it to do over again, I'd make sure we threw him a big appreciation dinner before he passed away, so he and others could hear the words of gratitude and admiration so many of us would want to share.

Another Civil Rights Movement leader in our county was Mitchell Hayes. Mr. Hayes was a little bit scary—he carried a knife, and we all believed he would use it—so when he spoke, people moved. In addition to his own efforts, he shuttled other people to and from meetings so they could be involved as well. Along with Mr. Rubin, Mr. Hayes spearheaded the group that guarded the Perkins home because of the threats made against Rev. Perkins and his family.

Jesse Newsome and Joe Paul Buckley were actively involved in the Movement as well. Mr. Newsome traveled the half-hour from New Hebron to attend meetings, even though he knew driving alone at night greatly increased his risk of being killed. He would also load up his truck and carry people to the voter registration office. Mr. Buckley, who was a faithful participant in local community-based civil rights activities, was one of the men arrested along with Rev. Perkins in Brandon ten years later.

The president of our local NAACP chapter was a man from D'Lo, the town where Dolphus grew up. His name was Ethel Lee, but everyone called him "BaBa" (pronounced bay-bay). Mr. Lee worked tirelessly to bring justice and opportunities to his neighbors in Simpson County.

Also important were those who couldn't participate openly in the Movement, but found ways to support it from behind the scenes. Mr. and Mrs. Dave Smith sold John Perkins the land on which he started Voice of Calvary Ministries. Mrs. Smith and some of the other ladies in the community were prayer warriors, interceding faithfully for the Perkins family and the mission. Many of these women worked for white folks, so they had to be very careful about their connection to the Movement.

Each of these people had a real influence on those of us who were coming up behind them. They showed genuine courage, risking their own lives and livelihoods so others could have a better life. They taught us that we had to stand up in order to make a difference.

Their example helped us to be strong when we faced danger ourselves.

About a decade after the "drive-by" incident at the Perkins home, Dolphus and I had a scare at our own house. We had two young children by this time, and Dolphus had taken over leadership of the ministry from Rev. Perkins. We had out-of-town guests staying with us the night we received a surprise visit from Mendenhall's one black police officer.

He banged on our door until we opened it. "Get your family out, get 'em out now," he said urgently as soon as we did. "They're gonna come and shoot up your house tonight." He didn't offer any kind of protection against the threat, and I doubt the other officers even knew he had come to warn us. This officer had limited authority—he wasn't allowed to arrest Whites—and many Blacks thought he'd been hired specifically to keep the police informed about goings on in the black community. Whether or not that was true, I was grateful that he was in a position to alert us to the danger we might be in.

We had to make a quick decision about whether to stay or to go. We sent the kids to stay with friends, but we and our guests remained in our home. Concerned about bullets coming through the windows, Dolphus and I moved our mattress to the floor. Our guests chose not to take that precaution.

We've always been blessed to have neighbors who looked out for us. The community rallied around us when they learned about the warning we'd received. One man even offered to lend us his shotgun.

"We already have a gun," Dolphus told him.

When our neighbor saw the hunting rifle Dolphus had recently bought, he laughed. "That's no gun!" he told us. "That wouldn't even hurt a squirrel." While we appreciated our friend's concern for our well-being, Dolphus chose not to borrow his gun.

In one sense, nothing ended up happening that night. No shots were fired. I don't know if anybody came anywhere near our house with intent to harm us. We'll never know if the whole thing was a hoax, or if the would-be shooters changed their minds at the last minute.

In the interest of full disclosure, I should tell you that Dolphus and I remember some of the details of this incident differently. How and when we first learned that a threat had been made, where the children slept—on some of these points, our recollections aren't the same. I've narrated the event the way I remember it. Where our memories converge is around the fact that this incident was one more in a long line of experiences that left us feeling unsafe and unprotected because of the color of our skin and our desire to be treated as equals.

People have widely varying opinions about how much Mississippi has or hasn't changed in the decades since the Civil Rights Movement. Some say nothing's really different— sure, the Jim Crow laws are off the books, but there's still plenty of racism, discrimination and segregation to go around. Others insist that the whole mess is behind us. Yes,

Mississippi used to have a race problem, but we dealt with it, and now we're doing just fine.

Many of us believe that the truth lies somewhere between those two extremes.

My first response, when somebody asks me how much things have changed, is to think about the ways that Mississippi really is different today than it was 40 or 50 years ago. African Americans can now go anywhere they want to eat (and enter through the front door). They can hold all sorts of jobs, can vote, and can run for (and win) political offices. Several cities in Mississippi have had black mayors, we have black representatives in our State Legislature, and we've even sent an African-American representative to our nation's capital. There are black judges and black attorneys, and a much greater (though still imperfect) sense of justice in the justice system.

Churches are much more open now, too. I can walk into just about any church I want to—including some whose Deacons used to stand at the doors to prevent Blacks from entering—and worship. People of different races can gather for honest conversation and not be persecuted—or prosecuted. Not only are people allowed to gather now, but people want to gather now. There's an openness to cross-racial friendships that didn't used to exist here. In some ways, I would even venture to say that Mississippi is now ahead of other parts of the United States with regard to race relations, simply because we recognize the problems of our past and are making the effort to have meaningful dialogue with one another.

On the other hand, I sometimes confront attitudes that have not changed much in the last few decades. Especially among the older generation, there are some white folks who would like for things to return to the way they used to be.

Sometimes, as we saw a while back with our state flag referendum, they want to hold onto symbols of the old way of life—symbols that may just say "Southern heritage" to them, but that say "slavery" and "segregation" to black folks. So while we are marching in a good direction, we also still have a ways to go, and things to work out.

One time, quite a few years ago now, but well after the days of marches and boycotts, I went into a store uptown. As I prepared to check out, a white boy approached the counter with a toy and a piggy bank full of change. The clerk reached around me to serve the boy first, taking the time to help him count out the coins he would need to complete his purchase.

This kind of thing happens at banks, as well. I will have been the first one waiting, but the teller, wanting to acknowledge the white person who came in after me, will say, "Who's next?" It's an awful feeling that goes over you when something like that happens—a sense of still being a second-class citizen even after all these years and all that struggle.

One time, I couldn't keep quiet. I asked the teller outright, "Why did you say that? You knew I was here first." She didn't answer, just turned bright red and got busy working on my transaction.

I guess I should be grateful. Another woman, coincidentally also named Rosie Camper, had a much worse experience at one of the local banks. She was waiting in line when a merchant walked in and stepped in front of her.

"Excuse me, I was in line first," that Rosie said.

The merchant hit her so hard he knocked her down. Rosie wore a neck brace for years after that. When the merchant went up to the window to do his banking, the teller told him, "I'm so sorry you were inconvenienced." The merchant never faced any consequences for the assault.

To me, the most heart-breaking place to encounter old ways of thinking about race is in the church. In 1990, I was reading my local paper and saw an announcement for a Bible study to be held at one of Mendenhall's prominent Protestant churches, on the white side of town. The notice said that women of all faiths were welcome. "Praise God!" I thought as I prepared to dial the number. I was looking for a Bible study at the time, and this one seemed like it would be not only spiritually beneficial, but also a chance to be part of something historic and exciting.

A very nice-sounding woman answered my call. I told her I was interested in the Bible study listed in the paper. "What's your name?" she asked me.

"Rosie Weary."

There was a long pause.

"Hello," I said. "Are you still there?"

"Where do you live, Rosie?"

That's when I knew there might be a little problem. "Well, I live across the tracks, in the quarters."

"Rosie, are you colored?"

"I'm black. Does that matter?"

She hesitated for a moment. "I don't think they allow Coloreds in their church." There was another pause, and then she offered a suggestion: "Maybe you could go to Jackson. I think they are accepting Coloreds in their Bible study."

Apparently, if I had been a white Mormon or Buddhist, I would have been welcome at that Bible study. As a black Christian, I was not.

This was certainly an upsetting and humbling experience for me, but God used it in positive ways in my life, and I'm grateful for that. For one thing, He gave me compassion for that woman who was defending a policy she might or might not agree with, but had no real power to change. I was reminded that racism imprisons all of us—not just those who are directly oppressed by it. He also challenged me to examine my own heart. "Lord, if I ever have negative feelings toward someone else based on race, please forgive me," I prayed.

The Bible study experience and others like it have made me even more appreciative of the white people I've known who were brave enough to challenge society's expectations.

As early as the 1970s, in Mendenhall, a bank teller named Vera Robinson always made black customers feel just as special as white customers. A real people person, she was always kind and friendly to everyone. I saw her very recently, and she hasn't changed a bit.

Of course, there were also the white volunteers who came from all over the country to work alongside us at Voice of Calvary (later called The Mendenhall Ministries). These men and women were willing to struggle for change (and sometimes risk their lives) in a community that wasn't even their own. Many of these volunteers have become life-long friends of ours, whom we stay in touch with and visit whenever we're in their part of the world.

One such precious gem is Chris Erb, who spent five or six years in Mendenhall. Chris not only made great contributions to the work of the ministry, but she was also generous, kind and wonderfully supportive of Dolphus and me as we were beginning our married life and growing into our roles as adult leaders in the community. She was the one who first helped Dolphus work on his book. People had been telling him for ages that he needed to share his personal story, as well as the story of The Mendenhall Ministries. Chris spent hours and hours with Dolphus, interviewing him and putting together an early version of the manuscript. When Bill Hendricks came along later and said, "There's a book here in Mendenhall," Dolphus agreed.

"Yes, there is," he said, "and we have a draft of it right here."

Lynn Farris first came to Mendenhall with a short-term volunteer group. She returned to spend a year with us, then went on to Fuller Seminary. She served for a while as one of the pastors at National Presbyterian Church in Washington, D.C., and invited Dolphus to perform her installation service, even though we're not Presbyterian. Later, she asked him to visit the congregation as a guest preacher at a Sunday morning service. Lynn's father served on The Mendenhall Ministries' Board.

Then there's the Rhine family. Margaret has brought volunteer groups to Mendenhall for 25 years, and her daughter, Sarah, spent time with us as well. Drs. Kevin Lake of California and Bob McElroy of Kansas both came and served at our health center on a volunteer basis.

And there are so many more. I wish I could name them all, but if I tried, I'd likely find myself in the same boat as John the Gospel-writer: "even the world itself could not contain the books that would be written" (John 21:25b).

Given our state's racial history, developing deep friendships with Mississippi Whites could be challenging, so we're particularly grateful for the Southern white men and women who have befriended our family. Many years ago, through an organization called "Faith at Work," Dolphus and I got to know several local white families: the Baileys, the

Parkers, the Ridgways, the Stovers, and the Myerses. The Baileys are a Jackson couple who reached out to us at a time when cross-racial friendships weren't at all popular in our state. Their believing that a relationship with us was worth having, even if it cost them something, has been a great gift.

Guy Parker grew up in my home town of Pinola (the fact that he and I can be friends today is a testimony to the fact that Mississippi has, indeed, changed). Guy's wife, Judy, wrote one of my favorite books, *The Stars Shone In My Hands*. Judy has an impressive grasp of the Word of God, and she also recognizes her own background of privilege. God has used her mightily as she has shared the things He's taught her. Guy has served on the Boards of both The Mendenhall Ministries and the Rural Education and Leadership (R.E.A.L.) Christian Foundation, which Dolphus and I began in 1998. In addition to being part of our ministry efforts, the Parkers have been faithful friends to our family, and have always been there for us when we've gone through hard times.

Louis and Helen Ridgway are businesspeople who also became dear friends of our family. For some reason, our son, Reggie, when he was in the hospital, always asked for shrimp. The Ridgways would go out of their way to bring a shrimp dinner to his room when they came to visit him. Howard and Flo Stover, and Barbara and Fred Myers, likewise became good friends as well as supporters of the ministries Dolphus and I have been involved with. All of these friends have consistently demonstrated genuine concern for our family's well-being, and their kindness to us and our children has touched us deeply.

And, there are Dr. and Mrs. Jim Baird. Dr. Baird served for over a decade as the pastor of First Presbyterian Church in Jackson, and he was always open to African

Americans being part of that congregation. He had fairly recently retired when Dolphus and I left Mendenhall, and we asked him and his wife if they would be spiritual advisors to us. They agreed, and they have been an incredible blessing to us in the years since, gracing us with their wisdom and hospitality.

As I look back over my journey thus far, one of many things I am truly grateful to God for is the fact that He has been both generous and creative when it came to my personal and spiritual growth and development. He has sent quite a collection of amazing people—black and white, male and female, from Mississippi and not from Mississippi—into my life to help me understand what it means to be a child of God, a disciple of Christ, and a laborer for the Kingdom.

Chapter Five
Walking With God: From church to conversion to discipleship

Even though I grew up going to church and Sunday School, hearing Bible stories and fiery sermons, watching my neighbors in the pews be overcome by the Holy Spirit, and participating in all the routines and rituals of a Christian congregation, I was in high school before anyone really explained to me what it meant to be a Christian. Sure, I'd heard all the stories from the Bible about men and women who walked with God, but somehow I hadn't come to understand that there was a step I needed to take myself.

I didn't know that I could have a personal relationship with God through faith in Jesus Christ.

But then John and Vera Mae Perkins moved back to Mississippi from California, and they started coming to speak at our school chapel services. They used Child Evangelism Fellowship materials—little fuzzy-backed figures stuck to flannel boards—to present the gospel simply and clearly. They made the same Bible stories I'd heard for years come alive. And they talked about needing to know Christ in a personal way.

Now I was hearing about salvation, but I didn't respond right away.

That didn't happen until my senior year, when Rev. Perkins invited a missionary named Bessie Rice to be a guest speaker at chapel. Somehow, even though she was using the same materials we saw every week, Mrs. Rice just made it so plain, talking to us about how baptism and church membership weren't enough—how we each needed to have our own relationship with Christ.

When she got done speaking, Mrs. Rice gave an invitation, and I wanted to go forward to accept Christ as my savior, but, like so many times before, I didn't. This time, though, I felt convicted about my inaction. After chapel, I stood in the middle of the schoolyard, beating myself up for not making a public profession of faith. Then I saw Rev. Perkins and Mrs. Rice starting to drive away, and I flagged them down.

"I want to give my life to Christ," I told them.

They were delighted, of course, and they prayed with me right there in the schoolyard. Rev. Perkins invited me to come to Voice of Calvary's Bible study in Mendenhall. My friend, Carolyn, had gotten involved with the Perkins family and their work some years before I did (kids at our school often called her "The Preacher" because she was constantly talking to people about Christ), and she already attended the VOC Bible study. When I mentioned to her that I'd like to go to the study but didn't think I would be able to because I didn't have a way to get there, Carolyn asked her parents if I could ride along with them. The first time I attended the Bible study, an invitation to discipleship was issued, and I stood up. My understanding of Christianity to this point had involved doing things, so I figured asking Christ into your heart was something you had to do on a regular basis as a Christian. Rev. and Mrs. Perkins explained to me that I had already accepted Christ, and, quoting Hebrews 13:5b, they assured me that He would never leave me or forsake me. That verse has stuck with me to this day.

The following summer was when I really got involved with VOC's ministry. Through Bible classes, the Sunday School Institute, Camp Cedine, and conversations with Dolphus, Carolyn and others, I grew in my understanding of the Christian life. Those weeks at Voice of Calvary also prepared me for the leap of faith I would take when I headed off to a college on the other side of the country with only $9.00 in my pocket.

As I consider that plunge and some of the other significant steps of faith I've taken over the course of my life so far, I see how many of the opportunities I've had to trust God have required self-sacrifice and the willingness to face some of my deepest fears and insecurities.

Attending Alcorn on a full scholarship certainly would have been a safer—some might say wiser—choice than departing for California before I even knew if I'd been accepted at Los Angeles Baptist College. Through my own hard work, I had prepared a way for myself that was well-paved and clearly lit. I probably would not have struggled as much academically at Alcorn as I did at LABC. As Alcorn is an historically black university, I also wouldn't have faced the difficult racial dynamics involved in life at a predominantly white college. I definitely wouldn't have endured the financial hardship and uncertainty.

On the other hand, LABC is where Dolphus and I started dating, got engaged, and began our married life. It's where I met Betty Wagner and Muriel Hamlin, who would overwhelm me with their generosity and become lifelong friends. It's also where I had an amazing opportunity to study the Bible and learn more about this Jesus in whom I had decided to put my faith.

In hindsight, it's easy to see that the cost of *not* stepping out in faith could have been much higher than what I sacrificed by going.

At the time, there was no way to know how things would turn out; there was only this new and exciting sense that God was leading me a certain way, and all I wanted to do was follow. Honestly, I don't think of myself as having been brave or even especially faithful. I think to a certain extent, I just didn't think. If I had really considered the whole of what I was about to do, I probably never would have gone to California.

But my faith was new and fresh, and I just knew God would lead and provide.

He did both of those things, and this is perhaps the most valuable thing I gained from my college experience: the opportunity to see God at work, giving me guidance and providing for me through His people. Because He took care of me then, it was easier for me to believe He would take care of me when I came to the next place where a step of faith took me in a surprising direction.

Deciding to marry Dolphus and agreeing to return to Mississippi with him both took me away from the paths I had thought I wanted to follow. My hopes for a secure life with a wealthy husband, my dreams of modeling—these were the things that competed with God's leading when I came to those crossroads.

Once we were married, Dolphus and I soon came to another set of divergent paths. We had agreed beforehand that we would not try to have children the first year we were married. After that year was up, Dolphus was ready to start our family. I was not. This was not a disagreement I had anticipated, and I remember thinking, "Wow, this is not going to be as easy as I thought."

My reluctance to take this next step was two-fold. For one thing, I once again faced the prospect of limiting my opportunities. There were still things I wanted to do, and places I wanted to go, before having children. My other struggle was my sense that I still needed to grow up first. I had helped raise my younger siblings, so I knew how hard it was to take care of children, and I just didn't feel like I was ready to jump into that.

Besides, I carried inside of me much of my mother's low sense of self-worth. I worried about whether I would be a good mother, and I was afraid that I would pass on to my children the same self-doubts that she had passed on to me and my siblings—the very self-doubts with which I was struggling at that moment.

For better or worse, I had also inherited my mother's aversion to confrontation. It was important to Dolphus that we start our family—many of our friends were having children at that time, and he was a few years older than I was (and probably feeling like he wasn't getting any younger)—so I soon gave in.

I didn't get pregnant immediately, but toward the end of the summer of 1973, I began to feel nauseated on a regular basis. When I went to the clinic we had recently started in our community and told my symptoms to our nurse, Joan Huston, she started grinning.

"I bet you're pregnant!" she said gleefully. I took a test, and sure enough, I was.

When I shared the news with Dolphus, he was ecstatic. By this time, I had gotten to the point where I was happy to know we were going to have a baby, but that wasn't my only reaction. I was still scared, too.

As with my choice to go to Los Angeles, this was a situation where the moment of decision wasn't really the step of faith. Sometimes, it's our faith that helps us make a major decision—the choice to accept Dolphus's marriage proposal was one of those. Other times, our decisions have different motivations—youthful enthusiasm, ignorance, not wanting to fight—and our faith comes into play as we live out the consequences of these choices.

I love all of my children dearly, and I am grateful beyond words to God for blessing me with each of them. However, I'd be lying if I said that being a parent was easy for me. Having children and trying to be a good mother to them has required huge amounts of courage and faith, and sometimes the enormity of this step nearly overwhelmed me.

Our firstborn, daughter Danita Ronique, was a beautiful, healthy baby whose birth on April 19, 1974, followed an uneventful pregnancy. But Danita was a screamer, crying almost constantly, and in addition to wondering if I would ever get any sleep again, I worried that she cried because I didn't know how to take care of her properly. To this day, I wonder whether it was just her nature, or if I was doing something wrong. Maybe I kept her too bundled up— dressing her as my mother had dressed us, when we lived in drafty houses with no heat.

Two years later, when our son Reginald Demond (Reggie) was born, things went less smoothly. After he'd been home for two weeks, Reggie developed a high fever and spent eleven days in the hospital with what the doctors thought was probably meningitis. That was a brutally hard experience, and I found myself unable to stay in the hospital with him—he had an IV in his head, and I could barely stand the sight of it. I came to see him every day, and Dolphus and Danita made several visits to the hospital as well, but in hindsight I wish I had been strong enough to stay with him. I think about how alone he must have felt.

Those days were hard for Danita, too. She had been so excited about having a little brother or sister, and she didn't understand why the baby had to go back to the hospital. As difficult as the experience was, though, it also contained a hidden blessing, as we saw our community pull together, everyone praying that Reggie would be okay, making sure Danita was looked after, and otherwise caring for us as a family.

Once Reggie got better and came home from the hospital, he was a happy baby, though he never was a good sleeper. We called him our "special boy" because we knew how easily we could have lost him right there at the beginning.

Despite the fact that things had turned out all right, and Reggie was now home and healthy, I found myself struggling with depression in the months after his birth. I didn't know what to call it then, I just knew I was tired all the time, I wasn't really interested in doing anything, and in particular it was hard to go to church. Worship didn't excite me any more, I couldn't pray, I wasn't interested in reading my Bible—it was a spiritual drought unlike anything I'd known since becoming a Christian.

One Sunday morning, our pastor talked about the importance of personal devotions. Specifically, I remember him exhorting us to read Scripture even if we didn't understand it, and even if we didn't feel like it. So I went back to reading my Bible and a devotional book that someone had given me. At first, it was just words on the page—nothing really registered. But as I forced myself to keep reading, day after day, I started once more to encounter God through His Word. I began to come back to life, and my faith became vibrant again.

Since that time, I've occasionally gone through similar dry spells. In fact, I experienced one as recently as the fall of 2009 (around the time I began work on this book, as a matter of fact). I don't panic now when I find myself in one of these spiritual rough patches, because I know that God can and will bring me through. That doesn't mean they're easy or pleasant. But as I read God's Word, whether I want to or not, I pray the words of a verse Dr. Richard Patterson (my wonderful history professor at LABC) and his wife once shared with me—"Cause me to hear Your lovingkindness in the morning" (Psalms 143:8)—over and over again until He does. Most recently, it was as the holidays approached, and I was reading the book of Romans, that God renewed my faith and joy in knowing Him.

For many years now, I've been the primary driving force in our family in terms of devotions, but that was a role I had to grow into. It has always been important to me that we spend time with the Lord, together as well as alone, but we used to go to family conferences, where we were taught that the man should be the spiritual leader in the house. So naturally I thought Dolphus should lead our family devotional times, as well as the prayer times he and I had traditionally shared before going to sleep at night. Whenever we got away from either or both of these routines, my response would be to press Dolphus to start them up again. But he had another idea.

"Rosie, I'm on the go so much of the time. Why don't you take the lead on this?"

We went back and forth on this for a while, but eventually I saw the wisdom in what he'd suggested. Dolphus was away a lot, traveling for the ministry. There was no reason our family's spiritual life should be put on hold until he returned. Even when he was home, he spent long days leading others in discipleship and ministry; why shouldn't I share in the responsibility of keeping our family focused on God and the work He had entrusted to us?

So I began to take more initiative. I did my own Bible studies, independent of anything we might be doing as a family, and I've now gone through the Bible several times. I also started waking the kids up early in the morning so we could read and discuss Scripture, and pray together, before they went off to school.

I heard a pastor tell a story once that made me feel better, knowing Dolphus and I weren't alone in having to work out how to balance spiritual leadership roles in our home. This pastor shared how his wife used to suggest that they pray together, expecting him to take the lead in making it happen.

"You know, I thought I'd married a woman mature enough to think and pray for herself," he said on one occasion, getting tired of her nagging, I suppose. He had no idea how much that one sentence was going to change their life.

Now his wife, in addition to praying on her own, goes around the world doing various types of ministry.

Sure, she still checks in with him. "Honey, is it okay if I go to South Korea?" she asked him once.

"We don't have the money," he replied, not really wanting her to go that far away and thinking she'd be discouraged by the lack of funds.

She came back with, "Okay, but if I get the money, can I go?" And sure enough, she came up with the resources she needed and took the trip, while her husband stayed home.

I haven't gone that far (literally or figuratively), but I am grateful that Dolphus pushed me to take greater responsibility for my own spiritual growth, and for leading and instructing our children in matters of faith.

After a while, our children grew from a pair to a trio. We call Ryan our "bonus baby," and God truly did surprise us with him. Danita was 13, Reggie was 11, and I was working full-time when I once again found myself feeling tired and nauseated day after day. Every evening after work, I collapsed on the couch and fell asleep. Even after two previous pregnancies, I didn't recognize the signs. I soldiered on, thinking I had some sort of bug, or was maybe just suffering from fatigue.

Eventually, I went to the doctor, and he ran some tests—I was so exhausted, I didn't even ask him what kind of tests he was doing. So you can imagine my confusion when he came back into the exam room and said, "Congratulations!"

"For what?" I asked him, still not getting it.

Finally, I came to understand that I was having another baby. Needing some time to get used to the idea, I didn't tell Dolphus about the pregnancy immediately. As Christmas approached, and my initial shock began to move toward joyful anticipation, I thought about creative ways to let my husband know our family would soon be increasing in number.

I bought some baby items (diapers, safety pins, etc.), wrapped them, and gave the present to Dolphus privately. It took him a minute to make sense of the strange gift, but soon he had figured it out, and he was thrilled. Dolphus had always hoped to have more kids; I was the one who originally thought two was enough.

Before Danita was born, Dolphus and I agreed that we would not name any of our children after ourselves (there were already three Rosies in my family, and Dolphus had unpleasant memories of being called "Doofus" as a child). We decided instead that each of our children would have one name that started with a "D" and one that started with an "R."

We gave Danita and Reggie the task of choosing a name for their baby brother or sister, following these guidelines. Now that I think about it, we took a bit of a risk doing that, but they came up with Ryan Donché, which we were perfectly happy to call our third child.

Ryan was jaundiced as a baby, but after spending a few days under a "bili light" at Simpson General Hospital and outside soaking up sunlight, he was fine—a good-natured child and the best sleeper of all our kids, at least at night. Naptime was another story, but, well, that's another story.

As I had after Reggie's birth, I struggled with postpartum depression after Ryan's arrival. I still didn't know what to call it, but I remember just sitting around while my sister Esta came over and bathed Ryan. She and a dear friend of mine, Miss Almeda, would clean the house around me as I waited, like the psalmist, for God to bring me out of the pit and set my feet on a solid rock (Psalms 40:2).

Eventually, I started feeling better, but that was another difficult season—another time when I had to trust God because I didn't have the strength or understanding to help myself.

Sometimes, depending on my mood, I look back over my life, and it seems like I've spent all my years just moving from one fear to the next. From my childhood fears of snakes, drowning and ghosts; to my anxieties about money and grades in college; to the terrors of the Civil Rights Movement; to uncertainty about getting married and having children; to the worst one of all—the possibility of losing a child—there's always been something to be afraid of, or afraid about.

Even today, after God has shown Himself faithful time and again (including when every parent's worst nightmare became reality for Dolphus and me), I sometimes find myself responding to situations first out of fear, and only later out of faith. My most recent struggle involves Dolphus's desire to move back to the country. One aspect of my fear is very basic: safety. While Dolphus maintains a busy travel schedule, I worry about being alone in an isolated place for extended periods of time. I've long said that I would only consider a move back to a rural area when he stopped traveling so much.

But there's more to it than that. There's security. Though I don't consider myself materialistic, I do resist the idea of letting go of some of the things God has blessed my family with. We don't live in a mansion by any means, but I could barely dream, as a little girl growing up in poverty, that I would someday live in a home such as ours: spacious, attractive and climate-controlled. Our home sits in a neighborhood filled with similar homes, and we are comfortable in this house and this community.

I try to justify my reluctance to move: "It's taken me all these years to get my dream home, I just want to spend a little more time here. I'm not ready to leave. Not yet."

But then God reminds me of all the ways He has provided for me over the years. All the ways He has protected me, comforted me, and guided me. I know what God has done in the past. Now I need to believe that He will be just as faithful in the future.

As I ponder these things, I am reminded that this life isn't about houses or other possessions, and it's not about being able to predict or control what lies ahead. It's about believing that God will go with me and take care of me wherever I am, and whatever my circumstances might be.

Because I do believe those things, I find myself moving toward being able, once again, to say to God, "If you want me to go, I'll go." Stepping out in faith does become easier the more you do it. When you've seen God do big things, you know He can handle the smaller things. Still, sometimes it takes a moment, for me, at least, to gather my courage and take another step down a road whose destination is unclear, and whose terrain looks like it might be dangerous or difficult.

In my experience, one of God's most precious gifts to us, as we seek to walk well with Him, is the companionship of others who share our faith. Among many such people in my life (including my husband, about whom I'll talk more later), I am deeply grateful for the friendship of one of the most godly women I know, a lady named Virginia Walker.

Virginia grew up in Oklahoma. In school, she studied to be a nutritionist. From her mother, she learned everything she needed to know to become a gourmet cook and baker. Out of her love for Jesus, she became a student of the Bible (I know several preachers who call and ask her for Scripture references on a regular basis) and a lay minister who loves and serves everyone she meets, including those one might call her enemies. Virginia makes people feel special, no matter where they are in life, and she is always available if anyone needs anything.

Virginia met Dolphus's friend, Jimmie, when they both worked with Campus Crusade for Christ in California. When they decided to get married, Jimmie invited Dolphus to be in the wedding. Even though Virginia and I didn't know each other well at that point, she asked me to participate in the ceremony as well. In the late 1970s, Jimmie and Virginia moved to Mendenhall (they each worked at The Mendenhall

Ministries for a while), and Virginia and I have been close friends ever since.

I couldn't begin to estimate how many hours the two of us have spent praying together and talking about the Lord. And I'm not the only one who loves to hear Virginia's perspective on spiritual matters—locals and volunteers alike flock to the ladies' Sunday School class she attends at Mendenhall Bible Church. They know they will receive sound Biblical insights from a knowledgeable woman when they sit in a classroom with her.

Unassuming in appearance, Virginia stayed home to raise six children, four of whom have completed college, and two of whom are still in school. One daughter, Erica, graduated at the top of her class at Simmons College in Massachusetts (with a double major in math and economics), and at her commencement, she received the college's top academic honor. Virginia almost wasn't able to attend the ceremony, because she had health problems that kept her from traveling long distances by car, and flights were too expensive. I hated the idea of her missing this special event, so I called John Perkins and asked if there was anything he could do to help. He had enough frequent-flier miles to get a ticket for Virginia, so she flew to Boston, while the rest of the family drove. Erica is now working on a doctoral degree. Another daughter, Lori, received degrees from Vanderbilt and Brandeis Universities. While still in high school, Lori went to the library and researched boarding school programs. She received a scholarship to attend the prestigious Dana Hall School in Wellesley, Massachusetts, and completed her high school education there.

By her example and her counsel, Virginia has always challenged me to strive for excellence, both intellectually and spiritually. When Danita and Reggie were young, and Dolphus was on the road so much of the time, and I struggled with my fears, Virginia shared Scripture with me and encouraged me to trust God. She would quote the Psalms: "I will both lie down in peace, and sleep; for You alone, O LORD, make me dwell in safety" (4:8). And I would believe her, and rest.

The privilege of worshipping alongside someone who lives out her faith as beautifully as Virginia does is one of many reasons I'm grateful to be part of the group of Christians known as Mendenhall Bible Church (MBC). We are a relatively small congregation—I'd estimate about 100 members—but MBC's influence is international. Rarely does a week go by when we don't have visitors—volunteers coming to help with the work at The Mendenhall Ministries, or people who heard about what we're doing and just wanted to see it for themselves. I am humbled and honored every time I learn that our efforts at ministry and discipleship have encouraged, inspired or challenged someone else. And I love meeting these brothers and sisters who come from far and near to worship with us.

As evidence of God's sense of humor, and to demonstrate how He has transformed me over the years, I'll tell you that one of my favorite parts of our Sunday morning service is when we sing a song called "Let's Rejoice and Praise the Lord." As we sing, we move about the sanctuary, greeting old friends and first-time visitors alike, and following the directions in the various verses of the song, including "shake a hand," "give a smile," and "hug a neck." Far from the threatening exercise this would have been for me years ago, this ritual has become a special and cherished part of our weekly time together.

Another thing we do every Sunday is reaffirm our congregation's mission statement: "We exist for the purpose of worshipping God, making disciples and reaching the total human being locally, nationally and world-wide." Once the formal service concludes, a core group of us stick around and visit—catching up on each other's weeks, discussing the sermon, making plans for upcoming church events or smaller get-togethers, and otherwise sharing life with one another. Our church is made up largely of extended, close-knit families. The downside to this is that any time one of our families has an out-of-town reunion, there's a significant drop in church attendance that week. One upside is that it's easy for us to think of all our fellow church members as family, so there's a wonderful depth to our relationships, and it feels natural for us to take care of one another in times of need or struggle.

Artis Fletcher has been our pastor almost from the beginning, and he is an excellent minister. A powerful preacher and teacher, Pastor Fletcher presents material in such a way that his listeners can easily understand what is going on in the text. He often preaches in series, working his way through a book or topic and helping us as a congregation understand more and more about how we are to worship God, love one another, and serve our community. I still remember well a series he did on the book of Nehemiah and the rebuilding of the wall of Jerusalem—a particularly useful study for a group of people committed to developing and uplifting their community. More recently, he presented a series on praise and worship, from the book of Psalms. He shared about his own journey of learning to worship God more openly and fully, and he encouraged all of us to apply these beautiful passages to our own lives as well.

Over the years, I've served in a number of roles at MBC, including church secretary, choir member, Vacation Bible School teacher, and Sunday School teacher. Many of my children's friends came through my Sunday School class (I taught third and fourth graders), and I loved having that time with them and getting to share with them about God. Unfortunately, I fear my students thought I was pretty boring much of the time. I'm not a dynamic speaker or outwardly emotional, so it could be hard to hold their attention and make them understand how much I cared about the things I was telling them.

In the end, though, it wasn't boredom, but rather a very different kind of reaction to my instruction, that brought my career as a Sunday School teacher to a close—or at least an extended hiatus. One week, I was talking about Moses as a baby, and about how his older sister had to help protect him because Pharaoh had ordered that all first-born Jewish sons be killed. There were several sibling pairs in my class, including two white boys who were visiting from Jackson. In an effort to give a sense of urgency to the lesson, I used them as an example.

"You wouldn't want someone to kill your little brother, would you?" I asked the older of the two.

He immediately started crying.

"No, no, that's not going to happen," I assured him frantically. "I just wanted you to understand how serious a situation it was."

As soon as class was over, the boy ran to his mother, and within moments, she was looking over at me like she wanted to shoot me.

Of course, I felt terrible. I knew I had made a mistake, and I wanted to talk to the boy's mother and try to explain what had happened. But I just didn't have the energy. Besides, I didn't have any idea what I would say to her. That's when I realized I was burnt out and needed to take a break.

What encourages me, as I look back on that season of my life, is to remember that Sunday School wasn't the only context in which I interacted with many of these young people. Because they were my children's friends, they spent hours upon hours in my home. I looked after them, prepared snacks for them, organized sleepovers, and otherwise welcomed them into our family circle.

To this day, some of those "kids" still call me Mama and come to me for advice or just to visit from time to time. They remind me that there are many ways to serve God and minister to others—though I may have had some less than stellar moments as a Sunday School teacher, that doesn't mean I wasn't teaching young people about God, and about how those of us who believe in Him are meant to care for one another.

I think about the verse from 1 Corinthians: "If the whole body were an eye, where would be the hearing? If the whole were hearing, where would be the smelling?" (12:17). If Dolphus and I were both charismatic speakers, always in demand and on the road as much as we were at home, who would have spent all those hours offering hospitality to our young neighbors? It's taken some time, but I have learned—and am learning—to value the kinds of gifts God has given me, and the opportunities (sometimes seemingly small) He's given me to use those gifts for His Kingdom.

Chapter Six

Utility Player For the Kingdom: Filling the roles that needed to be filled

Most of us, if we ask God for direction for our futures, probably hope that He will point down a long stretch of straight road ahead and say, very clearly, "Go this way." We also hope that every so often, signs will appear alongside the path we've chosen, confirming that we are getting closer to our intended destination. We long to be confident that we're going in the right direction, and it's a nice bonus if we can go in the same direction long enough to get good at it.

And perhaps some people experience God's leading that way.

I haven't.

Instead, my adult life has been a series of zigs and zags—less like an Interstate highway and more like a winding mountain road, filled with slow climbs, sharp descents and low-visibility turns.

Reviewing the journey from the 60-year mile marker, there are two statements I can make with certainty. It hasn't been what I expected. And, God has used the twists and turns to teach me about Him, to bless me, and to bless others through me in ways I never could have anticipated.

When Dolphus and I returned to Mississippi in the summer of 1971, I was diverging from my earlier plans of making a life and career for myself in California, and I had made my peace with that choice. What I hadn't realized was how difficult simply completing my college education would become as a result of our move.

The timing of our return made sense for both Dolphus and Voice of Calvary. Dolphus had just graduated from seminary and was ready to dive into the expanding work in Mendenhall. When integration had finally come to Mississippi in 1970, many black students needed help catching up to academic standards at formerly white schools, especially in math and science. So VOC organized after-school tutoring clubs to supplement its Bible studies and other youth activities. The ministry had also collaborated with the NAACP, the Civic League and other community groups to launch housing and farmers' cooperatives.

In fact, from Voice of Calvary's perspective, we were returning not a moment too soon. John Perkins was still recovering from his beating and subsequent surgeries, and he planned to move his family to Jackson as soon as he could transfer the reins of the ministry to a new leader.

For me, the timing was a little less ideal. I had just completed my junior year at Los Angeles Baptist College, and I had no intention of getting that close and not receiving my degree. I decided I would transfer to Jackson State College (now Jackson State University) and finish up there. Jackson State, however, wouldn't accept all of my credits from LABC. I wouldn't have to go all the way back to the beginning, but I would lose a lot of time, and I wasn't willing to do that.

So, I returned to California for my senior year, while Dolphus stayed in Mississippi. I saw him once that fall, when he came to Los Angeles to be part of a film (called *Too Late to Wait*) that Campus Crusade for Christ was producing. Being apart for so long early in our marriage wasn't easy—and apparently I didn't hide that fact very well, because some of the school officials at LABC felt sorry enough for me that they waived a few requirements and offered to let me take my final semester's courses (all electives) at Jackson State.

I was grateful for that accommodation, and I did what they suggested. I received my degree from LABC, with a major in history, a few months later. I didn't return for the commencement ceremony, though. It seemed silly to go all that way to walk across the stage when my family wouldn't be there anyway. What mattered was that I had finished. My parents were proud to have a college graduate in the family, and I felt a great sense of accomplishment, especially given all the different obstacles that could have kept me from getting to that point.

Then it was time for me to really settle into our life in Mendenhall. Dolphus and I were renting a two-bedroom house in the community, and I spent a lot of time there, either inside studying for the National Teachers Exam or out in the garden, tending my flowers. Like my mother and grandmother, I love beautiful flowers. I also found that gardening was a great way to get to know my neighbors, as we would exchange flowers, engage in conversation, and gradually develop relationships with one another.

Before it came time to take the test to be certified as a teacher, I arrived at another unexpected bend in the road. Dolphus and Rev. Perkins were now jointly running Voice of Calvary—Rev. Perkins commuted from Jackson and handled most of the fundraising in his role as President, while Dolphus, as Executive Director, was responsible for day-to-day operations. One day, they called me in for a meeting.

"We'd like you to work in the office," they told me. What they wanted was someone who could serve as a secretary for both of them, handling scheduling, phones, correspondence, etc. During my high school years, I had developed good typing and business skills, and they thought I was the right person for the job.

I was torn. On one hand, I had been involved with Voice of Calvary's work for several years, I believed in it, and Dolphus and I had returned to Mississippi so we could be part of it. Of course I wanted to be useful to the ministry, and to my husband and his mentor.

On the other hand, I had completed college so I could be a teacher. My mother was thrilled that I was pursuing that goal, and I felt like I would be letting her, as well as myself, down if I didn't reach it.

Then again, what I really wanted to do was whatever God wanted me to do. It's often hard to discern what that is, though, and in all honesty, I think I was listening more to Dolphus and Rev. Perkins than to the Lord when I said yes to their job offer. Of course, the counsel of godly people is an important part of seeking God's direction for our lives, but that doesn't mean it should take the place of our own prayer and discernment. If I had this decision to make over again, I would try harder to distinguish between the two and be sure that I had my own sense of God's leading before I moved forward.

At the time, though, I allowed myself to be steered into the role that Dolphus and Rev. Perkins thought was best for me. After all, I consoled myself, I don't have to do this forever. In fact, they had even presented the position as a temporary one when they offered it to me. I'd still have plenty of time to teach later, when someone else came along to take my place at the ministry.

So I became my husband's secretary, which introduced some complicated and challenging dynamics to our relationship. For one thing, always conscious of other people's opinions as I was, I worried that people might think Dolphus had married beneath him. Here he was, this rising star at the ministry, and his wife was "just a secretary." Like so many others, I fell into the trap of not properly valuing the work done by secretaries, assistants, and others who labor behind the scenes.

But there was more to it than that. Dolphus and I are different from each other in many, many ways, and one of those ways is our ability to compartmentalize. For Dolphus, work was work, and home was home. At work, I was one of several employees, and what happened there didn't have anything to do with how things were between us as husband and wife once we got home. For me, the distinction wasn't quite as easy to make.

If something happened at the office—especially, if Dolphus had been critical of my work performance in any way—I carried that home with me. I wouldn't confront him about it openly, but I would retreat into silence. Sometimes, noticing that I had withdrawn, he would ask me what was wrong. When I told him, he'd say, "That was just business," and expect me to switch gears and move on. He didn't understand why I was making things personal. Eventually, I stopped trying to explain what was bothering me.

Now, this is not to say that Dolphus isn't a good boss. Actually, he's a great boss. He's good with staff—he treats people fairly, he cares about them, he extends grace when mistakes are made, he's the first to go without pay when funds are short, and he's always had a deep passion for the kind of work we were doing at VOC. Dolphus cares deeply about the poor, and about people coming to know the Lord. Being at VOC was never just a job for him, it was truly a calling, and people have always respected him for the ways he sacrificed and labored to grow the ministry. And Dolphus's commitment to excellence is contagious—staff consistently gave him their very best because they saw and appreciated how hard he worked, and how he looked out for the people working alongside him.

Still, transitioning from wife to employee every morning, and from subordinate to partner every evening, was difficult for me.

So, for multiple reasons, I was relieved when I learned they'd found someone to replace me as secretary. "This is my chance," I thought, still hoping to pass the exam and launch my teaching career.

But by then, new things were happening at the ministry. Our youth outreach was flourishing—Herbert Jones would drive around the community, picking up kids and teenagers and bringing them to our Saturday night events. Before long, between Saturday nights and various weekday activities, about 150 kids were involved with the ministry's program. Because there weren't many structured ways for youth in our community to vent their energy, some tended to get into trouble. So we built a gymnasium. We'd open the gym in the evening and on weekends so the young people could come in and play ball.

Wanting to expand our activities further, we conducted community surveys, formal and informal, to learn more about people's concerns. As we did so, we discovered two major needs among our neighbors.

One was for educational services beyond tutoring. I remember visiting a family with ten children. None of the kids had ever gone to school, even though several of them were six or older. We couldn't do anything immediately, but we added "start a Christian school in the community" to our long-term to-do list.

In the meantime, we'd been reminded of another pressing need—health care. It wasn't unusual at that time for Blacks to sit all day in waiting rooms while white patients were seen first. Once, I took my mother to see the doctor, and we sat in the separate black waiting room from eleven in the morning (the time of her appointment) until five in the evening. When it became clear they were getting ready to close the clinic, I went up to the desk. "My mother hasn't been seen yet," I reminded the receptionist. They had completely forgotten about her. The doctor asked her a couple of questions and gave her a prescription for medication without examining her at all.

My mother wasn't the only one in the family to receive substandard care. My sister's son was born at an area hospital, where patient rooms were still designated "black" or "white." When my sister went into labor, there was no black room available, so they put her in a hallway. At least they took her to a delivery room to actually have the baby, but then they brought her right back out to the hall. The nurse even brought her a bedpan there and expected her to use it. If we hadn't been convinced before, we knew then that something had to be done!

So we started praying about opening a clinic that would provide quality health care to the members of our community. A couple from Pennsylvania, Erv and Joan Huston, had come to volunteer with us. Joan, a registered nurse, helped us with our planning and preparations. The Hustons stayed in Mendenhall for years, Joan working at the clinic, and Erv serving in Administration at the ministry. Later, Joan's sister, Mary, who is a nurse practitioner, came to help out at the clinic for a while.

It took a lot of hard work, and generous contributions of money, time and expertise from countless donors and volunteers, but we were finally able to open our clinic.

When we did, Dolphus told me he needed me to be the health center receptionist.

Once more, I faced that difficult choice: pursue my own goal, or put it on hold to play a supporting role in important work that was happening in my community. For multiple reasons, including the fact that I still wasn't good at speaking up for myself, I chose the latter, even though I was disappointed about missing another opportunity to become a teacher.

I want to be clear, in case anyone thinks I'm blaming my husband, Rev. Perkins, or anyone else for my inability to speak my own mind or make my own decisions at this point in my life. I'll talk more about the speaking my mind part later, but for now let me just say that no one forced me to make any of the choices I made. I was the one who went along with other people's suggestions, rather than putting forward my own thoughts about what God might have in mind for me. I take full responsibility for my lack of courage, which stemmed from a poor self-image. In fact, I think sometimes I even used the idea that "this is what 'they' want" as an excuse not to take riskier steps of faith.

On the flip side, I sometimes also used the fact that I hadn't "chosen" my role in the ministry as an excuse not to fully engage in the work I'd been given. Again, this was my short-coming, not anyone else's, and God dealt with me about it. He helped me to understand that even though Dolphus was both my husband and my boss, my primary responsibility was not to please Dolphus. My number one objective should be to please God in all I do, including work/ministry. Times when I got frustrated about the kind of work I was doing, when I thought, "Let Dolphus just fire me, then," it wasn't Dolphus or the ministry I was really letting down. It was God.

There's a concept that has been very helpful to me over the years. I don't know where it originated, but we heard it a lot of times at Faith At Work conferences we attended. That concept is: "Bloom where you are planted." In other words, wherever you are in life—whatever you are doing or whatever your circumstances may be—strive for excellence. It might not be clear exactly what you're supposed to be doing. Even so, you can continue to trust God and live for Him. Seek to please God in all that you do, and I firmly believe He will use you for His glory and either give you peace where you are or lead you on to where He wants you to be.

As I internalized this principle, and as I committed myself to serving God well no matter what role I was in (and no matter how I had gotten there!), God really did use my efforts to do good in the world. And He gave me a new understanding of what it meant to reach my full potential in Christ. It wasn't nearly as much about what I did as it was about how I did those things.

This has been a long process, and I can say with the Apostle Paul: "Not that I have already attained, or am already perfected; but I press on..." (Philippians 3:12). I'm grateful that God has brought me this far, and I trust Him to complete the good work He has begun!

By the time I began my new job as health center receptionist, Rev. Perkins had shifted his ministry focus to Jackson, and Voice of Calvary headquarters had moved to a rambling house on St. Charles Street, near Jackson State

University. Our organization became known as VOC-Mendenhall, and Dolphus now served as its President. Not only did this increase the pressure on Dolphus, but it also meant that suddenly he was traveling a lot, raising funds and awareness. This was difficult work, especially as many people around the country didn't understand the distinction between the two VOCs.

"John was just here," the folks at Channel 38 in Chicago told Dolphus when he tried to arrange a guest appearance on one of their shows. He explained the situation to them, but they didn't think their viewers would understand, and they didn't allow him to appear on the show. "People aren't going to remember 'Jackson' or 'Mendenhall,'" Dolphus was told. "They're just going to remember Voice of Calvary." To avoid more of this kind of confusion, we changed VOC-Mendenhall's name to The Mendenhall Ministries (TMM).

The other challenge Dolphus faced as a frequent traveler was that his busy schedule kept him away from his young family more than he liked. He decided we should travel together—him, me, toddler Danita, and infant Reggie. To keep costs low, as well as to nurture relationships, we almost always stayed with host families in the communities we visited. I love meeting new people, and I deeply appreciate the gracious hospitality shown us by so many, but bringing my young children into other people's homes was a tremendous source of stress for me. Even though the kids were for the most part very obedient, I still lived in constant fear that they would accidentally break something or cause some other kind of trouble for our hosts.

I'm sure I projected that stress onto Dolphus, but he felt it was important that people see us as a family, so we continued to travel together for years, and we both just lived with the silent tension it contributed to our relationship.

Children are more astute observers than we often give them credit for being, and Danita once made a remark about our family travels that caught Dolphus by surprise. In the early 1990s, Dolphus met a gentleman whose son would later become a professional golfer. This man told us that if we could get our family to Oregon, he and his family would take care of us there. A couple of years later, we bought our tickets and flew west. Dolphus made a point of leaving his briefcase at home. We stayed in our friend's mother's house in Eugene, our food was all taken care of, and we had a wonderful time. At some point, Danita said to Dolphus, "You know, Dad, this is the first real vacation we've had."

"What do you mean?" Dolphus asked. "We've been all over the country."

"Those weren't vacations," Danita, in her late teens at the time, asserted. "Those were PR trips."

Now that our children are grown, I love traveling with Dolphus. We've been all around the country and to several other parts of the world, and we have a wonderful time. We meet all sorts of people, experience different cultures, see what God is doing in communities near and far, and share about the important work we're privileged to be a part of in Mississippi. I attend Dolphus's speaking engagements, staff a small "booth" where we sell books and distribute information about the ministries we're involved with, participate in small group meetings, pray with Dolphus about the various events on his calendar, and make myself available for whatever needs might arise. If time allows, I might also ask someone from our host organization to point me toward the nearest consignment store, so I can do a little bit of shopping between events.

We still often stay in people's homes, but if we bring our young grandson with us, we generally get a room at a local hotel (my idea!). Occasionally we make exceptions, like when we stayed with a couple who lived on a farm in Iowa and had plenty of room for an active grandchild to play, or when we visited our good friends John and Margaret Rhine in Illinois, but for the most part, if there's a child on the trip with us, we stay in a hotel.

Although the traveling, fundraising and marketing during TMM's early days presented challenges, God gave us favor. One person or church would introduce us to another, and more and more people got behind the work we were doing—by coming to volunteer with us, supporting us financially, praying for our efforts, or some combination of those things. In addition to the health center, we launched Genesis One Christian School, a Community Law Office, and a number of other programs that expanded the much-needed ministry John and Vera Mae Perkins had begun with a handful of Bible Clubs back in 1960.

Over the course of nearly three decades at TMM, I filled a number of roles—basically, wherever I was needed, that's where I was. After serving for a while as the health center receptionist, I became a community health educator. Then I was Dolphus's secretary again, and for a while I worked as a nurse's aide. If the floors needed to be swept, or the bathrooms needed to be cleaned, I did those things, too.

One thing I never did, though, was teach, even though we eventually opened our own school. There were at least two reasons for my decision not to teach at Genesis One. One was that I'd done a little bit of substitute teaching in the public schools by then, and, to be honest, I was no longer entirely sure that teaching was something I wanted to do. In addition, by the time our school opened, Dolphus had a very heavy travel schedule. If I'd become a teacher, it would have been much harder for us to travel together as a family. While I served as his secretary, others could cover my office duties while we were away, and Dolphus and I could work together on various projects and tasks from the road.

Between trips, I also got many opportunities to exercise my gift of hospitality. When volunteer groups came to town, we used to have them over to our house for cookouts. After a while, that became a bit overwhelming, so we would invite them over for dessert instead. When individual guests or small groups came to visit the ministry, we had them stay with us.

Dolphus likes to call me his utility player. I guess that's a pretty apt description. In baseball, the utility player is someone who may not be a big star, but is valuable to his team because he can play several positions competently. My hope is certainly that I've done well those parts of the work that have been entrusted to me over the years, even if they seemed small at the time.

Come to think of it, it's mostly "small" things that I remember when I look back over all those years in ministry.

I remember two women from the community who used to come by the office to sit and talk with me, and to borrow money. These ladies' families were poor and down-and-out, and they said they liked visiting with me because I didn't discriminate—I treated them like I would anyone else. Whenever I lent people money, I told them they needed to pay me back before they asked for more. One of these women stopped coming around for years because she hadn't paid me back and knew she couldn't ask me for anything else. The other one always paid me back promptly, no matter what. She would walk through rain, or even one of Mississippi's occasional snows, to repay the loans (usually $15-20).

Not wanting to be concerned only with people's physical and financial needs, I always talked to these women about Christ when they came to see me. I never heard that either made a commitment to the Lord (one has since died, the other is still living), but I always hoped that at some point they would remember the things I'd told them and come to believe that God loved them far more than I ever could.

Then there were the elderly women who came to the clinic. I called them "pretty ladies" and always looked for something to compliment when they came in (which they did sometimes for an actual doctor's appointment, and sometimes just because they craved interaction with other human beings). They were so appreciative of my making them feel special that sometimes they'd bring me flowers or gifts to say thank you. One of these ladies loved trinkets, so I'd give her a little something every Christmas. It really didn't take a lot to make people happy. Just knowing that somebody noticed them and cared about them meant a lot.

Another older woman in our community, Miss Almeda, is a recovering alcoholic. A number of people from our church had talked to her about Jesus over the years, but it ended up being a volunteer from Seattle who led her to the Lord. Miss Almeda is still at Mendenhall Bible Church, and she has ministered to me in many ways over the years, praying for me, helping me around the house, or watching the children when I needed a break. She has a great sense of humor and loves to kid with people, so she keeps us laughing, but she also knows what she wants, and she doesn't mind bossing folks around a little bit. Especially when Christmas is coming—about two months ahead of time, she'll start dropping her hints. "These old socks, they're really startin' to tear up," she might say. For whatever reason, it's always socks that she wants. So every year, I buy her several pairs, in different colors and styles.

One of the things I especially enjoyed doing for the elderly women in the neighborhood was to bake up a batch of Mama's teacakes and leave them on their porches. One woman loved the teacakes so much, she would check her front porch every couple of days, just to see if I'd left any. I wrote about my "teacake ministry" in a *Daily Guideposts* article once, and I was astonished when I started getting letters from people all over the country in response. One woman asked for the recipe, and now she bakes them for people in her community. I never would have guessed that a simple little teacake could have so much of an impact.

Serving with The Mendenhall Ministries all those years, though it might not have been my first choice initially, was in the end a tremendous blessing for both Dolphus and me. Seeing God work through us, along with the rest of the staff and volunteers, to bring visible change in our community was incredible. And having the opportunity to develop relationships with so many wonderful people—our neighbors, those who came to us to help with the work, and those we met on our travels—has been, and continues to be, a privilege whose value I can't begin to measure or express.

Still, there came a point when we knew it was time to leave. We'd been on staff for close to 27 years by then. The ministry had grown tremendously (employing roughly 40 people and serving thousands), and Dolphus was raising funds from all over the country. All of our properties were paid for, and we had a reserve fund in the bank. On the surface, things were going incredibly well.

Underneath, though, there was tension. Not the kind of tension you get when people dislike or disrespect each other, but the kind of tension that results when two different philosophies of ministry collide under one roof—or, in our case, under two adjacent roofs.

On one side (and we never wanted for there to be sides, but it's hard to know how else to explain what happened), Dolphus, along with many of the ministry staff members and national members of the Board, saw TMM as an organization that had been commissioned by a local church (to do work beyond the scope of what the congregation itself could accomplish), but now "belonged" to a broader base of people who shared our vision and invested in our work.

On the other side, the elders and many members of Mendenhall Bible Church felt strongly that the ministry was the church's outreach arm, and that the church should have the final say in decisions about the work of the ministry. In 1997, many of the national Board members were replaced by local members, giving the church the majority voice on the Board.

Dolphus knew that it would be extremely challenging to convince national donors to give to the work of a local church. If he were to succeed at that, he would need to travel even more than the roughly 60 percent of his time that he was already spending on the road. Church leadership, though, wanted him to travel less, so he could use his teaching and leadership gifts more at home.

Dolphus and I began to discuss the possibility of moving on. I had been feeling for a while that God had some new things in store for us. And Dolphus was becoming convinced that it was time for one philosophy to function at

TMM/MBC—it didn't really matter which one. There were valid points on both sides of the argument, but the argument itself was holding the ministry back.

We prayed about it and decided, yes, it was time for a change. We didn't have anywhere else to go yet, but we were sure it was right for us to move on, and we trusted that God would provide for the next season in our lives.

Some friends of ours had counseled us that if we left, we should remove ourselves from the equation completely: Move out of the community, don't serve on any Boards there, and leave the church. We ended up following the first two parts of that advice, but not the third. We love our church—the people, the teaching, and so many other things about it—and once we had resigned from the ministry, and the church could take the work in the direction they wanted it to go, the tension we had felt before began to dissipate. We were no longer a threat to people there, and we came to feel a renewed freedom as we attended and worshipped alongside our brothers and sisters.

We didn't stay at the church just because being there got easier. Even before we knew that would happen, it had been important to us to demonstrate that people can leave something (the ministry, in our case) without being upset about it. That people can have differences of opinion—even the kind of differences that make it hard to work together—and still worship together.

And we still supported the ministry. We wanted to see it thrive—and since we no longer felt responsible for the organization's direction, we didn't need to argue with current leadership about the best way to make that happen. We could just encourage them to seek God and do what seemed best to them.

Though we did not leave the church, it soon became apparent that it would be wise for us to move from Mendenhall, as our friends had advised. While we stayed in the community, people—especially volunteer groups who came to town already knowing us or our story—continued to look to us for leadership. We wanted to clear the path for people to establish connections with the folks who were now running the ministry.

There was also a very practical reason for us to make a move. Dolphus had gotten a job in Jackson, some 40 miles from Mendenhall. Before we left TMM, Dolphus had already begun serving on the Board of Mission Mississippi, a statewide nonprofit organization dedicated to racial and denominational reconciliation. Lee Paris, the Chair of that Board, knew that Dolphus had been traveling and speaking about racial reconciliation, so as soon as he learned that Dolphus was available, he asked him to pray about the possibility of becoming Mission Mississippi's Executive Director.

For about a year, Dolphus commuted to Jackson every day. It was doable, but that was a long drive on top of long working hours, so we kept praying about—and looking for—a house closer to Jackson. It was hard, though, to find something that was in our price range and also met my primary criterion: It had to be at least as nice as our house in Mendenhall. Not that that house was luxurious, but we had made improvements to it over the years, and it was a comfortable home for our family. I didn't feel a need to "move up," particularly, but I did not want to go back down. So we looked for a long time, with no success.

And then, out of nowhere (from our perspective), God gave us a house. He really did.

There was a man whose church was partnering with an inner-city ministry in their area to build a Family Life Center. Someone gave him a copy of Dolphus's autobiography, *I Ain't Comin' Back*, and he read it. This man was serving as the liaison between his suburban white congregation and the inner-city black church they were partnering with, and hearing about Dolphus's life and the work of TMM helped him navigate the complexities of that role and the relationships involved. It gave him an understanding of black culture that he wouldn't have had otherwise, and that understanding helped him avoid some of the mistakes and miscommunications that often happen when people first begin to work cross-culturally. He was so grateful and encouraged by the whole thing that he just had to meet Dolphus. So he and a couple of other men from his church flew to Mississippi to meet my husband. That in itself was a little bit overwhelming!

Dolphus showed the men what Mission Mississippi was doing. They were impressed, but didn't ask how they could support the organization. So he took them to Mendenhall and showed them the work there. Then the man who had read Dolphus's book said he wanted to meet me. So Dolphus brought him and his friends to our house. My sisters, Esta and Earlene, were there with me when the group arrived. We all talked together for a while, and then Dolphus drove the visitors back to the airport.

Along the way, the man said, "You know, I already support other ministries. I don't really want to give to another one. I want to do something for you and your family. What does Rosie want to do? What is she dreaming about?"

When Dolphus told him about his commute to work and that we'd been looking for a new place to live, the man said, "That's it! I want to help you get a house."

He came down again not too long after that, and he and I went all around the area, looking at houses. We didn't find anything that seemed right for our family, so Dolphus and I thanked him for all his help, and he flew back home. Shortly after that, he called Dolphus. "Tell Rosie to find the house she wants," he said, "and I'll provide the down payment."

At first, I was reluctant to take this man's money. He was thinking about running for office, and even though it wasn't a local position, I didn't want to be indebted to a politician. But he promised that there would be no strings attached. He said this was just something God had put on his heart to do for us. So I agreed to let him help us. It was such an awesome gift that he was offering us, it really blew us away. For so long, we'd been busy meeting the needs of others. Now someone wanted to help meet ours, without asking anything in return.

It happened in kind of a round-about way, but we finally did find a wonderful new home. Every time we went out looking with our realtor, she'd say, "If we don't find you a house somewhere else, I'll take you to Southwind." But she never did. Southwind was always just someplace we could look if there was nothing else to be had.

Finally, we said, "We'd like to see Southwind." Southwind, we soon found out, was a predominantly white working-class subdivision. There were maybe three or four black families living there when we came looking for a house. We visited three properties that were on the market. None of them was quite right for us. As we were leaving the subdivision, we saw another "For Sale" sign, and we asked our realtor to make an appointment for us to look at that house. When she returned the next day to arrange our tour, a gentleman came over from across the street and mentioned to her that he was looking to sell his house. He hadn't put it on the market yet, but he was ready to sell, and he wanted to do it quickly. (The house, as I learned after we moved in, tends to be dusty, and his three daughters all have asthma.) Since this man hadn't yet engaged a realtor, he could offer us a good price. Our realtor set up an appointment for us to come look at that house, and that was pretty much that.

As I said, God gave us a house.

Southwind (located in the town of Richland, Mississippi) is very different from Mendenhall. When we moved in, the population was probably about one percent black. Today, I would estimate that African Americans make up approximately 25 percent of the community, but in the early days of our life there, I had to go out of my way to meet my black neighbors.

One day, as I was driving down our street, I saw an African-American woman working in her yard. I made a U-turn and stopped to introduce myself to Linda Jackson, who has since become a co-worker and dear friend. On another occasion, a black person passed me while I was out walking. I followed that person home and introduced myself.

In addition to the racial make-up of the neighborhood, there's also just a different feeling to this community. In Mendenhall, people sit out on their porches and greet everyone who walks by. It can get a bit noisy sometimes. Southwind, on the other hand, tends to be very quiet. It's a blue-collar community, primarily, and I guess people work hard, they come home, and they just want to be with their families. But since I refuse to not know my neighbors, I made an intentional effort to meet the people who live around me, white as well as black. I stopped by people's houses, bearing blueberries or baked goods, and I'm happy to say that most of the people I've encountered have been very cordial. Some have been downright welcoming.

It's quite possible there were those who weren't happy about our moving in. Besides the working families, a number of older Whites built their retirement homes here in Southwind, and they probably didn't expect a lot of Blacks to join them in their community. But no one has been hostile to us. And I've been proud to observe that the black families who live here have kept up their properties just as well as the white families. I think it's good for people to see that Blacks and Whites aren't necessarily different from one another in the ways they might expect—and that you can't judge how a person or family will behave simply by the color of their skin.

Of course, there are some people who believe that Dolphus and I deserted the black community by moving to a predominantly white neighborhood. I don't see it that way, though. Dolphus and I both grew up in low-income black communities, and then, as adults, we lived in one by choice for nearly 30 years. We were happy there, and if God leads us back, we'll go. We moved to Southwind because it was close to Dolphus's job and because we found a home here that we liked and could afford.

And God has used our Southwind experience in a number of ways. Not only have we, and the other African Americans in the community, been able to expand the horizons of some of our white neighbors, but I've learned some important lessons myself from being here. Perhaps the most important is that moving here didn't make me any different from who I was before. For such a long time, I thought it would. I dreamed of life in a nice, big house. I dreamed of the security and joy that would come with that house.

What I've learned is that things don't give you peace. God does. I am truly grateful to God, and to our generous brother in Christ, for enabling us to have this home. But it's my relationship with God that gives me peace. And it's the people in my life, rather than the things, that truly matter.

So we've really tried to use this house for God's glory, figuring if He didn't give it to us because we needed it to be happy, there must have been another reason, or reasons. One of those reasons, we soon discovered, was the apartment over the garage, in which we set up an office and started a small grant-making foundation.

I should back up a little bit. *I Ain't Comin' Back* was first released in 1990, a few years before Dolphus and I left TMM. Initially, proceeds from book sales went toward an endowment for Genesis One Christian School. Once we moved on from the ministry, we thought we should use the book-sale income differently. Not that we had anything against Genesis One, but we thought if we were funding it in such a substantial way, we would want to be involved in decision-making.

Dolphus and I are both passionate about racial reconciliation and rural communities, and as we thought about how to move forward in life after TMM, God laid it on our hearts to start a foundation that would support ministries in rural Mississippi. We would continue to sell Dolphus's book, but now the proceeds would endow our foundation—the Rural

Education and Leadership (REAL) Christian Foundation. It didn't take long to decide our roles.

"If you do all the speaking, I'll do all the work," I told Dolphus.

So I became REAL Christian Foundation's Executive Director (which mostly involved correspondence and maintaining a database), while he served as Chairman of the Board. We had wonderful volunteer support from the very beginning. Mr. and Mrs. Howard Holshuh came from South Carolina to help us out short-term, while our new neighbor, Linda, agreed to volunteer with us on an ongoing basis. Friends from TMM, Lisa Johnson and Billy Craft, helped us with our finances (such as they were)—setting up our books and laying the groundwork for stability in our record-keeping.

We began with 2,000 copies of *I Ain't Comin' Back* and no money. Dolphus was on several national Boards, so whenever he traveled to Board meetings, he would arrange speaking engagements in the area. He told people about our mission to "connect economic and technical assistance with rural ministries" and asked them to consider supporting us. We let them know that book sales supported our grant-making and encouraged each person who heard Dolphus speak to buy a copy. For those who wished to invest a little more, we suggested that they purchase additional books that would then be given to graduating high school seniors in small towns around Mississippi. Of course, they could also simply make a donation.

Not wanting to wait until we were fully endowed to begin giving, we made our first round of grants ($500 each to three ministries) during our second year of operations. Currently, we provide small annual grants and technical assistance to 13 ministries, and we hope to increase that number even more, although Dolphus and I have a slight difference of opinion about what our goal should be. He thinks we should support 20; I don't see why we should stop there.

Having worked at a rural ministry ourselves for so long, we know first-hand how difficult the work can be. We want to have a real impact in communities, so we do everything we can to train and empower the ministries we support. In addition to the grant funding, we provide training workshops and hold an annual celebration dinner. At this dinner, representatives from the ministries we work with have the opportunity to meet one another; form relationships; and exchange information about available resources, best practices, and other aspects of their work.

These gatherings bring great joy to my heart. It's exciting to hear about the things people are doing with limited means. And each year, we have performances or presentations by young people who are being served by the organizations. Seeing the children and youth up on stage, sharing their talents and testimonies, is truly inspiring.

In fact, there is very little about REAL Christian Foundation that doesn't inspire me. From our dedicated staff to the amazing people whose work we support, everything about our small foundation makes me more grateful than ever to God, who has blessed us so richly.

Our staff includes five people, if you count Dolphus and me (and I do, since REAL is my full-time job, and Dolphus now splits his time between the foundation and Mission Mississippi). Linda Jackson, who volunteered with us initially, is now a part-time employee. Linda is one of those people you want working for you—extremely conscientious, she'll keep looking for a missing penny until she finds it. She tracks all of our income and expenses, and she works with

Board member Mark Biggs (a professional accountant) to keep us in compliance with government regulations. She also works with the auditors each year. As long as Linda is around, we know that everything will be in tip-top shape. And not only is she a diligent worker, but she is also a great friend to our family.

Virginia Chase, who served as Dolphus's assistant at Mission Mississippi for many years, recently became a full-time REAL Christian Foundation employee. Virginia had helped us with our database from the beginning, but now she also keeps up with Dolphus's busy travel schedule, handles correspondence, and produces our newsletter. Virginia is great with computers, and she also relates extremely well to people on the phone. Everybody loves to talk to her when they call our office. In fact, I sometimes suspect they're a little disappointed if they get me instead.

Our other employee is a young woman named Crystal Cline. Crystal started volunteering with us while she was a student at Belhaven University in Jackson. She's now a graduate student at Mississippi College. Crystal works with churches and organizes Dolphus's non-travel-related activities. She's quiet, but very good at what she does, and we're delighted that she has chosen to continue working with us.

And then there are the laborers in the field. Please allow me to introduce you to a few of these faithful men and women devoted to helping young people who are growing up in terribly difficult circumstances.

One of our ministries, the Lexington Colts, is located in one of the top 10 poorest counties in the nation. About 60 kids participate in Rev. Willie Reeves's sports-based ministry—gaining skills, learning discipline, and imagining possibilities for their lives. Rev. Reeves starts working with kids when they are six years old, teaching them about the Word of God as well as instructing them in life skills and athletics, and he maintains relationships with many of them even after they leave his program at age 12. Quite a few of these young people have gone on to college; often, they are the first in their families to have done so.

We also support a small Christian school in Morton. A former Genesis One teacher, Mrs. Loreatha Kincaid, used to drive 30 miles from her home in Morton to teach in Mendenhall. She dreamed of starting a school in her own community, and she asked REAL Christian Foundation to help her. After beginning in her home with just a few students, she now runs the Alpha and Omega Christian Academy, which is attended by approximately 65 students, both black and white. Her teaching staff is also racially diverse. Mr. Kincaid, recently retired from his job as a school principal, now helps his wife run her academy.

Dolphus and I know Tony and Shannon Duckworth from our Mendenhall days. Dolphus mentored Tony, and Shannon worked at TMM. Now, through their Mt. Olive Ministries, the Duckworths work with young men who are at risk for becoming involved with gang activity or otherwise falling through the cracks. The ministry has a contract with the City of Mt. Olive to create PowerPoint presentations, so much of the focus of the program is on computer skills, but the youth also participate in Bible studies, receive tutoring, and study robotics.

In Tylertown, children flock to a church basement for one of the town's only after-school programs, sponsored by Jayess Christian Ministries. The kids take turns working on donated computers, and they are required to complete their homework before going outside for "recess." If it weren't for this program, run by Mrs. Alice Dillion, these young people might have trouble finding organized activities to participate in once school got out for the day (to our knowledge, the local Boys and Girls Club is the only other after-school option in the area). In addition to academic support, workers at the program teach the children about values and principles.

Through Young Life Delta, Quiana Head-Franks works with young ladies. Having been a rebellious teenager who became a mother at age 14, Quiana hopes to keep the girls she works with from going down the same path. She takes them to camp (outside of Mississippi, so they can see a little more of the world) and teaches them about Christ. Just recently, Young Life has asked Quiana to start working with local teen moms, as well.

Stories from the ministries we support through REAL Christian Foundation encourage and energize me—and I'm grateful for that, because I've found that ministry can be exhausting, discouraging work sometimes.

I don't know if it's because I've spent so much of my time behind the scenes, or if it's just my personality, or if this is something everyone in ministry struggles with, but I have to admit that there were many points along the way when I questioned myself and the work we were doing. In fact, there were probably more days when I wondered whether we were making a difference than there were days when I was sure we were.

Of course, we saw physical differences being made in people's lives, and we saw some people coming to faith in Christ, but still I found myself wondering, "Why aren't more coming to the Lord? Why isn't the community changing faster? What are we really doing here?" Maybe it's just human nature to want things to change overnight, to want everyone to embrace the work we do, to want to see all of our neighbors' lives change for the better, right away.

On a day-to-day basis, when you're in the thick of things, it can be so hard to see the fruit of your labor. People who came in from outside often saw things more clearly than those of us who were involved full-time could. It was obvious to these visitors that God was making a significant difference in a community, and in individual people's lives, through this team He had brought together.

To be honest, I thought frequently about quitting. I thought about going back to California, living for myself, getting a big house, and going into modeling, as I had once dreamed. But every time I started to get really tempted to give up and run away, the Lord would redirect my thoughts. Sometimes He would remind me that there were no guarantees about that glamorous path I'd thought I was going to walk. I might never have made it as a model. Or, I might have experienced some success, and then ended up dead in a ditch or on Skid Row. It happens. Other times, God would simply draw my attention to some of the good things that were happening around me—things I never would have seen if I hadn't been willing to move back to Mississippi and serve Him there.

I might stop by Genesis One and see the children there learning—getting an excellent academic education, but also learning about Christ. Many of those kids would go home and talk to their parents or other family members about God. Like Miss Almeda's nephew, Kenneth, who asked his family if they could start saying a blessing before eating their meals.

Or I would learn that one of the young people we had worked with had decided to live his or her life in a way that would benefit others. When Dolphus and I first returned to Mississippi, we served as youth directors at Voice of Calvary. We called some of the young people who were involved with the program then "our children," even though they were fairly close to us in age. We had special relationships with these young men and women, and they spent a lot of time with us in our home. Among this first generation of "our children" are Marlene Hardy, who is now a social worker at the Mississippi School for the Deaf; Larry Harper, who employs homeless men in his construction site clean-up business; Lynn Phillips, a physician who has built her practice in a low-income neighborhood in Jackson; Lynn's brother, Arthur, and his wife, Shirlene, who operate a plumbing business and often hire young men who've been in some kind of trouble and need a second chance; and Tracy and Keith Coleman, who live in Virginia and both work for the government (Keith is retired military and also an ordained minister).

When I think about these young people, now grown and giving so much to others, I realize that God always did want me to be a model. Not a fashion model, as I originally thought, but a role model in His Kingdom. The work isn't as flashy, but I can see now how valuable it is, and I realize I got a pretty good deal in the exchange of futures.

Time accomplishes many things, and I believe one of its gifts to me is that I can look back on Dolphus's and my years at TMM with a fairly balanced perspective. I see things we did well, and great things God did through us, and I also see things that I would do differently if I had the chance. I would be more interactive with people in the community, especially young people, and I would be bolder about talking to them about Christ. I would be even more concerned about their spiritual lives than I was about their academic success, and I would really encourage them to be all they could be for God's glory. We did a good job, I think, of welcoming into our home those volunteers and other visitors who came to us from afar. If I were doing it over again, I'd make a greater effort to also open our home to our neighbors.

I would spend more time studying the Bible. I might even lead a women's Bible study. I would be braver about standing up for what I thought was right, and for myself. I would follow some of my own dreams, and at the same time, I would make more of an effort not to take any of the people God has placed in my life for granted.

Including my own family. I think many of us have a tendency to get so involved in ministry that we don't do as well by our own families as we should. God blessed Dolphus and me with three precious children, and in hindsight it's easy to see how I could have given them more of my time and attention as they were growing up. I see God's grace in the fact that it's also easy to see evidence of His character in their lives. Each of our kids is very different from the others, but they have all demonstrated deep compassion and a willingness to give of themselves to minister to groups of people often neglected by the world at large. So when I think about opportunities I've had to serve God, and when I wonder whether my efforts have yielded good fruit, my own home is a good—maybe even the best—place to start.

Chapter Seven
The Home Front: Balancing family and ministry

It was an inauspicious beginning, to say the least. One week before Danita was born, there was a major flood in Mendenhall. Almost everything in the black part of town was affected, including Voice of Calvary's recently opened health clinic, where our brand-new X-ray equipment sustained thousands of dollars' worth of damage. As disheartening as that loss was, my attention was primarily focused on the disaster I faced at home.

We had over three feet of water in our house, and as it receded, a thick coating of mud remained on the walls and floor. I stood on the porch, nine months pregnant, and peered in at the mess. It was a horrible feeling, knowing that I didn't have a clean, safe place to bring my baby home to. I was in no condition to deal with the situation myself, so I petitioned the Health Department to clean and sanitize the house, but they said no.

As so many apparent tragedies do, this trial showed me how blessed I truly was. Even though their own homes were flooded, too, people from the community banded together to help Dolphus and me. They scrubbed and disinfected, making sure the house would be ready for its newest occupant.

Seven days after the flood, with Dolphus at my side, I delivered Danita at University Hospital in Jackson. A few days after that, we returned to Mendenhall, and the balancing act we'd had to engage in as spouses and ministry partners suddenly became even more complex.

I like to think that Dolphus and I have grown into our roles as parents reasonably well, but it certainly wasn't easy, and we both made our share of mistakes, especially early on.

Perhaps because Danita cried a lot and that concerned me, or maybe simply on account of her being our first child, I became pretty completely absorbed in caring for her and our home. I'm afraid I may have neglected Dolphus during those first few months—maybe longer. He probably felt a bit left out of the family he'd been so eager to start.

Then again, his conviction at that time that men shouldn't help around the house didn't help matters. The very thing that might have freed me up to pay more attention to him was something that simply didn't occur to him to do. At least, not yet.

After a few months, I returned to my job at The Mendenhall Ministries, and Danita went to daycare. Several TMM staff members had young children, and Harriet McKinnis looked after them on site, which was wonderful. Having Danita nearby, and under the care of someone we knew and trusted, made that initial separation less traumatic.

Reggie was born two years after Danita, and by now our balancing act was more like a three-ring circus. Dolphus was traveling constantly, it seemed, and that was a source of stress, whether we accompanied him or not. I've already talked about the difficulties of traveling as a young family.

But not going with him brought hardships, too. For one thing, of course, the kids and I missed him while he was gone. But every time he came back, even though I was glad to see him, I faced the disruption of many of the routines I'd established in his absence.

You see, Dolphus and I have some personality differences that had significant impacts on our child-rearing styles. I've always tended to be the stricter one, wanting to teach the kids discipline and manners, and preferring to have steady routines. Dolphus is much more laid-back, and his "let kids be kids" philosophy sometimes threw a wrench in my well-laid plans. Plus, he felt guilty about being away from the children, so he sometimes let them do things I'd specifically told them they couldn't—like stay up past their bedtimes watching television or playing games. When he'd leave again, and I'd try to return to the routines I had established, I could expect to hear complaints along the lines of, "But Dad let us..." So I'd be mad at him because he had turned me into the bad guy and then disappeared.

As I said, we both had some room for growth. Here's an example: For years, we struggled to be on time for church on Sunday mornings. I would get up and make breakfast for everyone, then I would wash the dishes (I always washed the dishes before church, because I never knew when Dolphus might spontaneously decide to invite someone home with us for lunch), and then I would get the kids ready while Dolphus got dressed. When it came time to leave, he would wonder why I wasn't ready yet. He might even get upset, because he hated to be late for church.

I don't remember exactly how long this went on (probably not as long as it seemed to me at the time), but one Sunday morning, I just said, "You go on, I'll walk over when I finish up here." And it was like a light came on for him, and he realized how much I was doing, while he'd just been taking care of himself. After that, he started cooking breakfast (grits are his specialty!) and washing the dishes, so I could get the kids and myself dressed and ready to go on time.

This same story speaks to an area where Dolphus helped me to grow. It could be a source of tension, this habit Dolphus had of inviting folks over at the last minute. Eventually I realized that it wasn't that Dolphus was being insensitive to the work he was putting on me, so much as that we just had very different ideas about hospitality. When people come over, I want everything to be perfect—a clean house, a complete meal, and so on. Dolphus is much more interested in the fellowship. We could have popcorn and water for refreshments, and that would be fine with him.

Now, I haven't come to the point where I'm willing to serve my guests popcorn and water. But I am grateful for the ways Dolphus has reminded me to cherish time with friends and family—to focus more on content, and less on presentation, if you will.

And even though it sometimes made things harder for me when the kids were young, I'm glad Dolphus is the kind of parent who really allows (and wants) his children to be themselves. He always made sure to tell them, especially Reggie as the older son, that they didn't have to follow in his footsteps. He never pressured them to carry on his legacy as a ministry leader. Nor did he insist that they be model children just because people might be watching. I was the one who felt compelled to make sure our children behaved a certain way because of who Dolphus was. I was the one who worried constantly about the spotlight that shined on him and caught the rest of us in its edges. I thought our family needed to be perfect, and I fear I stifled my children because of my own insecurities.

In almost every area of our lives, the same dynamic holds true: Dolphus is more laid-back, while I'm more tightly wound. The one time we switch roles is when we go fishing. For me, fishing is about the experience—enjoying nature, anticipating the tug on the line, even appreciating the silence and stillness between catches—and it's something I do to relax. For Dolphus, it's about catching fish. He needs a certain return on the time he invests, and if he doesn't start to see that return fairly quickly, he's ready to be done. The kids didn't ever really get into fishing, either—we took them when they were children, but they didn't like it much. Too many mosquitoes. So mostly, over the years, I've fished with my sisters, especially Vera. She and I have traveled all over with our rods and reels (though, truth be told, I still mostly use a cane pole, the way we did when we were kids).

To his credit, Dolphus keeps trying. During the summer of 2009, we visited a lake, owned by a friend of ours, that is stocked with large catfish. Dolphus had borrowed a special reel from this friend. And he was actually enjoying the outing, because he caught a big catfish early on. He had to really wrestle with it to reel it in. A little while later, he got an even larger fish on the line. While he was struggling with that fish, his cell phone rang. I had advised him to leave his phone in the car, but Dolphus and his cell phone are not easily separated.

"Don't get that," I warned him.

But Dolphus couldn't ignore the call. He let go of his fishing pole with one hand, so he could dig the phone out of his pocket, and the fish swam right off, dragging the borrowed reel behind it.

Of course, Dolphus felt terrible, and I insisted that he call our friend (who was on the road at the time) immediately to confess what had happened. As soon as Dolphus explained the situation, our friend began laughing. "That's happened to me, too!" he said. Then he told Dolphus that he had devised a way to drag the lake for reels that had been "stolen" by the big fish.

So no harm was done, but I imagine Dolphus will be even less inclined to go fishing with me now.

The intersection of ministry and family didn't occur only around the issue of raising children. In Christian community development, we talk a lot about the "felt need concept"—the idea that ministry should respond to the needs and issues that members of the community feel are most important and/or urgent. I've already shared about how the lack of quality health care affected members of my own family. Tragically, my mother died relatively young because of this need that had gone unmet for so many years.

Between being an only child (and therefore engaging in a lot of heavy physical labor that otherwise would have been done by sons in the family) and having ten babies, one right after the other, my mother's body had been through an awful lot by the time she reached middle age. She suffered from high blood pressure, fainting spells, and rectal bleeding for many years. Over and over again, she visited a doctor, only to be asked a few questions and sent home with medication—including Preparation H, because her colon cancer (an extremely treatable cancer in its early stages) had been misdiagnosed as hemorrhoids.

By the time we opened our health clinic, and a doctor actually cared enough to examine my mother and run some tests, the cancer had already spread and could not be effectively treated. She lived a couple of years after that, enduring multiple hospital stays, a colostomy bag, and a lot of pain. Mama spent the final week of her life at Simpson General Hospital, in a coma. Daddy was so distraught that he was hospitalized as well; his room was right next door to Mama's, and we children went back and forth, checking on them both.

Mama died the week Reggie turned three, with her husband and most of her children at her side. I remember feeling numb, and hollow inside, wondering how we were going to get along without her. I was sad that she wouldn't get to know her grandchildren, and that they wouldn't get to know her. I was also worried about how Daddy would manage on his own.

As it turned out, my father wasn't on his own for very long. I didn't know this at the time, but apparently several women took to calling him on a daily or near-daily basis pretty soon after my mother died. I know Daddy grieved her death, but he also craved companionship. Nine months after Mama passed away, Daddy announced that he had gotten married to Ms. Gussie Gray. I knew Ms. Gussie a little bit—her children had come to programs at VOC, and Dolphus had gone to high school with one of her sons—and she seemed like a sweet woman. I was happy for Daddy—glad he didn't have to be alone, and glad that the person he'd chosen to spend his later years with was someone with a kind heart. It took some of my sisters a little longer to come around. They didn't have anything against Ms. Gussie, particularly; they just thought it was too soon for Daddy to remarry. "Mama's not cold in her grave" was a refrain I heard often for a while. Daddy and Ms. Gussie were married for almost 20 years, until she died.

After that, my father's health began to decline (not surprising, as he was in his late 80s by then). He had poor circulation, and eventually one leg had to be amputated. He was 92 at the time, and he had kept driving almost until the day of the surgery. He would have found a way to continue driving even after that if we had let him. Eventually, we didn't feel comfortable with his living alone any more, and Daddy moved in with my sister, Esta. When problems arose in his other leg, he refused amputation and developed gangrene. He spent his last few months in hospice care, in a lot of pain. And it seemed like he was just so tired.

We always sang when we visited Daddy at the hospice, and he generally kept us laughing in spite of everything, but not that last Sunday. He couldn't sing, and we knew he must be in terrible pain. He kept looking at a wall, as if he saw somebody there. I believe He was looking at Jesus, and that he was ready to go home to the Father. I thought about staying with Daddy that night, but we had our grandson with us and needed to get him home. The next morning, just before she left home to visit Daddy and feed him his breakfast, my sister received a call from the hospice staff that our father had passed away. I felt bad that none of us was with him in his final moments, but I do trust that the Lord was present, and I believe that was a comfort for Daddy.

As we had for Mama, we held a "celebration service" rather than a traditional funeral for my father. We wanted our time together to be upbeat—a real celebration of his life—and Dolphus led the way in that, keeping everyone in stitches as he delivered a eulogy filled with funny stories about Daddy. The grandchildren sang beautifully at the service, accompanied by my sister, Elizabeth, on the piano.

A special blessing for us that day was the presence of two of Daddy's grandchildren who didn't ordinarily participate in our family gatherings. His grandson, Elliott, surprised us by coming down from Illinois for the service. Elliott hadn't seen Daddy since he was a little boy, so it touched us deeply that he made the journey to say good-bye. There was also a granddaughter, who lived in Los Angeles, whom Daddy hadn't even known about until five years earlier. The two of them loved each other immediately when they met, and she had been back to visit him at the hospice just a few weeks before his death.

I know I'm not alone in having regrets about things I didn't say to my parents before they died. I wish I had really expressed to them how much I appreciated everything they did for me and my siblings. I wish I had told them how much I loved them. Especially Mama. With Daddy, there was more time, and we did talk about some of these things. But Mama— even though she was sick for a long time (or maybe *because* she had been sick for such a long time), her death felt like it came suddenly. I didn't really believe she would go so soon, and I hadn't thought through what I wanted to be sure to say to her while she was still with us. Plus, Dolphus and I were traveling a lot at that time, and we had two small children. There's no doubt in my mind that the work we were doing was important, but I still wish I'd made more of an effort to spend time with my mother during her final years.

Similarly, I know that I am in the company of many parents when I fret about all the things I could have done better in raising my children. Even the specifics of my list probably resemble the litanies other parents recite. I could have spent more quality time with the kids—reading, listening, allowing them to share what they were going through, doing creative projects together, and so on. I could have insisted they spend less time watching television and playing video games. I could have preached less and encouraged more. I should have given them more room to be themselves, to make their own mistakes, to learn and grow by trying things on their own. If I had it to do over again, I'd work on those areas.

But there's another list, one that I hope matters more. On this list are all the things Dolphus and I were able to do for, and give to, our children. Things like talking to them about the Lord, praying together, and going to church together. Things like hugging them and telling them we loved them (I'm so grateful Dolphus and his family taught me to do these things!). Teaching them to respect and care for others. Encouraging them to reach their potential and follow their dreams. Involving them in the ministry we were privileged to undertake over the years.

As much as it exhausted me at the time, I'm even glad we were able to take the kids (and occasionally some of their cousins) with us on our travels. I never left the state of Mississippi until I was in the eleventh grade. By the time my children were that age, they'd been all over the country. Danita and Reggie even enjoyed taking trips by themselves. (Ryan didn't like the solo travel so much; after one such trip, he decided he'd rather only go places with the rest of the family.) We'd put them on a plane, and they'd spend a few days with family friends or at some summer program or another before returning, full of stories about the people they'd met and adventures they had. (Reggie, if I'm honest, occasionally went overboard in the meeting people and having adventures department—he called from an airport once, while on his way to Kamp Kanakuk in Missouri, to inform us that he'd missed his connecting flight because he'd met a white boy who was also on his way to a summer camp, and they'd lost track of time while they were talking.)

Perhaps, though, you'd prefer to "meet" my children rather than wade through any more inventories of my parenting strengths and weaknesses. I pray that as you learn about each of them, you will experience just a bit of the profound blessing they have been to Dolphus and me.

The Same, Only Different: Danita

Of all my children, Danita is the most like me: quiet, shy, studious. Other than attending her high school prom, she didn't really date or party as a teenager. When would she have had time? She was so busy studying hard, winning awards, and paving the way to attend college on a full academic scholarship.

That said, there's some of Dolphus in Danita, too. Like her father, she has the kind of intelligence that makes her well-spoken and quick on her feet in a conversation, even in an argument. (While I do fine with book learning, I've never been able to express myself as articulately, especially off-the-cuff, as those two can.) And speaking of arguments, Danita doesn't mind standing up for herself. She does it respectfully, even quietly, but she does it.

I'm so glad Danita has this self-confidence, because even though she grew up after the Civil Rights Movement and its social justice-related achievements, she has still faced many challenges as an African-American female in the South. Some of these challenges she kept secret for years, preferring to handle them herself rather than trouble Dolphus and me with them. Only recently, for instance, has she told us about ways the administration at her integrated public junior and senior high schools attempted to limit her accomplishments.

Danita was incredibly well-rounded as a student. Not only was she involved in a number of extracurricular activities—SADD, math and science clubs, and the bands (she played clarinet in the marching band, baritone sax in the concert band)—but she also excelled in all of her academic subjects.

Her first year at Mendenhall Junior High, Danita won all four academic awards offered by the school—math, science, English and history. It's possible race wasn't a factor in what happened next, but it's also possible the administration wasn't comfortable with the idea of a black student taking home all those prizes, because the following year there was a new rule: no one student could win more than two awards. Since Danita had again qualified to win all four, she had to pick which two she would accept. A couple of years later, about the time Danita graduated, this rule was reversed.

Danita continued to flourish in high school, winning more awards, scoring a 30 on her ACT exams, and generally being a star student. Despite her strong academic record, her guidance counselor suggested she go to the local Vocational-Technical Center to take some classes. Had Danita heeded this counselor's advice, she wouldn't have had enough academic credits to attend college when she graduated from high school. She also wouldn't have been valedictorian of her graduating class. I can't see any logical reason for the counselor's suggestion, so I have to assume that racial bias, if not outright racism, was involved.

Fortunately, Danita had the common sense to say no to the counselor's bizarre suggestion, and she did graduate as valedictorian of her class. Even so, most of the academic scholarship offers she received (including those from some Christian colleges she was considering) were partial, often covering less than half of her costs. She could have taken a band scholarship, but she didn't want to.

Then Rhodes College in Memphis offered her a full academic scholarship, as well as a Bonner Scholarship, which provided a stipend for community service. Danita decided to attend Rhodes and volunteer at a local soup kitchen.

In college, Danita faced what I and so many other Mississippians had also struggled with: the disparity between Mississippi's and other states' educational systems. Her high school classes had not adequately prepared her for college. (Dolphus and I, seeing that she wasn't being fully challenged by her high school courses, had sent Danita to Colorado one summer for supplemental classes in math and Latin, but even so, she had some catching up to do.) Never one to shy away from a challenge, Danita worked harder than ever and did well enough in college to be accepted to medical school at the University of Tennessee in Memphis. She planned, at that point, to become a psychiatrist.

While in medical school, Danita met a doctor couple and babysat their child regularly. The wife, a Neonatologist, sometimes invited Danita to come to the hospital with her. Before long, Danita had modified her career goal: She now wanted to become a pediatrician.

As a medical student, Danita once again found herself facing a double dose of discrimination—as a black person and as a woman. The way she describes it is that she felt invisible. Instructors often ignored her, directing their questions to others in the class. That bothered Danita. "I wanted to say, 'Hey, I'm here, and I have a mind, too,'" she's told me—after the fact, of course. Danita handles herself well, and I'm sure she dealt with the situation effectively (she did, after all, accomplish her goal of becoming a pediatrician), but it grieves me that she had to fight to be fully included in her own education.

For all the advancements we've made, and we have made many, racism and sexism remain serious problems that affect many aspects of our society. I hope and pray that any granddaughters Dolphus and I may one day have will experience educational, professional and social environments that are more inclusive and supportive than those our daughter navigated.

I am incredibly proud of Danita. Not only because she has overcome such long odds and daunting obstacles to become a physician, but also because she is a generous and compassionate human being. Pediatricians don't make as much money as some in the medical profession, but Danita didn't select her specialty based on financial considerations; rather, she chose it out of genuine concern for children and their health. She has returned to Mississippi and practices in Natchez, where she bought a home a few years back. She contributes freely to REAL Christian Foundation and the other ministries we've been involved with as a family.

Sometimes, looking at what Danita has accomplished does remind me of my own long-ago career dreams. From time to time, I wonder what might have happened if I had made different choices. But I'm not jealous of Danita for doing what I didn't. Dolphus and I always said we wanted our children to be able to go beyond what we had done. I'm thrilled that my daughter was able to pursue (and attain!) her dream. Besides, looking back, it's easy to see God's hand on both my meandering back road and Danita's determined climb toward a specific lofty destination.

Our Special Boy: Reggie

I've already told you how Dolphus and I called Reggie our special boy because we nearly lost him when he was a baby. That nickname took on a double meaning a few years later.

About a week before Reggie's seventh birthday, we took a family trip to Estes Park, Colorado. Reggie had come down with a cold before the trip, and he was still a little stuffed up. While we were in Colorado, his congestion got worse, and then much worse. One night, I had to sit up holding him because he was having so much difficulty breathing.

We drove to Dallas, where Dolphus was scheduled to visit a local church to preach and teach a Sunday School class. During the Sunday School hour, we shared with the class about what was going on with Reggie. After church, someone came up to us and told us that there was a member of the church—an Ear, Nose & Throat specialist—who would be willing to see Reggie that afternoon. He wouldn't charge us anything, except a quart of Blue Bell.

We had no idea what Blue Bell was.

We asked around and found out that it was ice cream. So we got hold of a container of vanilla Blue Bell ice cream and took it with us to the doctor's office. He gave Reggie some medication and instructed us to see the doctor at home as soon as possible. We went to Show Biz Pizza Palace that afternoon to celebrate Reggie's birthday, then drove the rest of the way home and made an appointment with our family physician, Dr. Dennis Adams.

Dr. Adams, a young African-American physician, had come from New Jersey several years earlier to serve as the full-time doctor at our health center in Mendenhall. He had first learned of the clinic when he heard Dolphus speak at an event in Newark. At the time, he was nearly finished with medical school, and he was wondering where he could use his gifts and training—he didn't want to go overseas, but he did want to serve in a community that really needed him. He thought our health center might be the right place for him and his family. They moved down as soon as he had completed his residency. The Adams children grew up in our community and have been good friends of our kids. Dr. Adams continues to work at TMM's health clinic to this day. His wife, Judi, was instrumental in getting Genesis One Christian School off the ground and served as its first administrator.

Dr. Adams prescribed additional medications, but I still had to hold Reggie all night so he could breathe.

So Dr. Adams sent us to a pediatric ENT in Jackson, who in turn referred us to a hematologist at the University of Mississippi Medical Center. The hematologist couldn't figure out right away what was wrong, so he admitted Reggie to the hospital. Dolphus stayed with him that night, and I returned the following morning.

For four days, the doctors ran tests. Starting around the second day, I began to hear people using words like carcinoma, biopsy, etc. I recognized these terms from my work at the clinic, and I told Dolphus, "They think our baby has cancer."

Dolphus's first response was, "You don't know what you're talking about." He wasn't trying to insult my intelligence; he just didn't want to believe that Reggie could be that sick.

On Thursday, we got the results of the biopsy: Non-Hodgkins Lymphoma.

Denial soon gave way to a rush of different emotions, including anger at the apparent injustice of the situation. "We're in ministry, doing God's work. This isn't supposed to happen to us," I remember thinking.

I stewed in my righteous indignation until I looked around at the other kids, and the other moms and dads, going through similar ordeals. As I observed their suffering, the question turned itself around, from "Why us?" to "Why not us?"

"Why do we think we're so special?" I asked Dolphus at one point. "Those parents are asking the same questions. They're hurting just like we are."

The doctors, who were still trying to figure out the best way to treat Reggie, wanted to put him in a national study. Participants would receive either just chemotherapy or chemotherapy and radiation simultaneously, based on a random drawing. We weren't sure what to do, so we consulted Dr. Kevin Lake, a member of TMM's Board of Directors, who was on staff at the University of Southern California Medical Center. He spoke favorably about the study, and also about UMMC's pediatric cancer department in general. He said the treatment Reggie would get there would be just as good as, if not better than, what he would receive anywhere else in the country. So we agreed to participate in the study. Dolphus, who had heard negative things about radiation treatment and didn't want to see Reggie go through that, hoped he would draw "just chemo." I, on the other hand, thought "the more treatment the better." If one method didn't get everything, maybe the other one would. I wanted Reggie to get both.

He got both.

Dolphus was right about this part: It was terribly hard to watch Reggie go through those treatments—both types of treatment. Early on, the chemo made him very sick (though later rounds would only affect him for a day or so each time), and after a couple of treatments, his hair began to fall out. Dolphus asked if we could shave his head, and Reggie said yes.

In addition, there were spinal taps, medication injected into the spine, and bone marrow tests, all of which were very painful procedures. The bone marrow test was the worst. The staff wanted Dolphus and me both to stay with Reggie while they administered the test. I tried, but I couldn't take it. I ran out of the room. I just couldn't watch my son suffer like that.

Besides the physical pain, we feared that Reggie might face emotional pain in the form of teasing from the other children when he went back to school. We shouldn't have worried. When he returned to Genesis One, the kids welcomed him back enthusiastically. Under the guidance of his teacher, Marlene Hardy, they had been praying for him and had also put together a book of get-well wishes to present to him on his return.

While he was still in the hospital, Reggie was a source of inspiration to everyone he interacted with. He was the one encouraging Dolphus and me to keep up hope, and he also made a mission out of cheering up the other kids on the ward. The doctors and nurses adored him, even though he did cause a bit of trouble with his antics. He would often sneak out of his own room to visit his fellow patients, and he'd try things like skating down the hallway with his IV pole. One time, a nurse came to give Reggie his medications, and he was nowhere to be found. It turned out he and another child had snuck down to the morgue.

We'll always be grateful to those medical professionals who took such good care of our little boy. In particular, I'll never forget nurse Betty Gentry, who would sit in a chair and rock Reggie when he was in pain or couldn't get to sleep. There was also a particularly tall physician, whom the kids (and adults, for that matter) called Dr. Tree. Dr. Tree took some of her young patients to baseball games and even invited them to visit in her own home.

Reggie was in the hospital for ten weeks. During that time, he received cards and notes from people all over the country who were praying for him. By the time we got ready to take him home, the walls of his room were completely covered with these greetings. One friend, knowing that Reggie's favorite professional football team was the *Pittsburgh Steelers*, sent a *Steelers* jersey, hat and other gear. Volunteers working with TMM stopped by to visit, as did many of our local friends and neighbors, both black and white.

In addition to the tremendous emotional support our family received during this time, God also took care of the finances. Dolphus had fairly recently gone on staff at Piney Woods School. One of the things this meant was that he had double health insurance. He'd been planning to drop his policy through TMM, but hadn't done so yet. Between the two policies, Reggie's medical expenses were completely covered—which was a good thing, since we didn't have any money to pay medical bills.

We also had help from a group, called Candlelighters, that reaches out to cancer patients. Not only did this organization pay for the kids in the ward to have television service in their rooms, but they also contributed funds to cover the gas it took to travel between Mendenhall and Jackson for follow-up appointments after Reggie was released from the hospital.

After the ten weeks of his treatment were over, Reggie never stayed in a hospital again. He had check-ups every week at first, then every two weeks, then every month… Five years after his diagnosis, he was pronounced cancer-free.

There was another positive outcome of Reggie's hospital stay. Dolphus and I had talked to him many times over the years about our religious beliefs, and Reggie knew all about the Christian faith, but he hadn't made a commitment of his own to Jesus. While he was being treated for lymphoma, our long-time friend Carolyn Fletcher shared the gospel with Reggie, and he accepted Christ. Dolphus and I were delighted that our son, during such a difficult trial, chose to reach out to God and believe in Him.

Reggie flourished in the wake of his bout with cancer. He finished elementary school at Genesis One, then moved on to Mendenhall Junior High, and then to Mendenhall High School. Though he didn't apply himself quite as much as he probably could have, Reggie was still an honors student. He participated in a number of sports (basketball, football, even tennis for a little while), played drums in the band for a short time (until he discovered he couldn't be on the football team and in the band simultaneously), joined a few clubs, and was very popular with his fellow students. I was extremely nervous about Reggie playing football. One of the effects of the radiation treatment was that it stunted the growth of his neck. Because of that, I was terrified that someone would tackle him and snap his neck.

So I was relieved when, of the various sports he tried, basketball was the one Reggie really excelled at. By his junior year, he was the starting point guard on the school team. He wasn't the best shooter on the team, but he could move the ball and get it to the people who could make the baskets. Dolphus and I were proud of what a great team player he was, and we attended almost all of his games, even those that were out of town. During Reggie's senior year, Dolphus intentionally arranged his travel schedule so he wouldn't miss games. I know it meant a lot to Reggie that his father made a point of being there in the stands, cheering for him.

Reggie also continued to relate well to young children. He worked at TMM during the summers, and he was like the pied piper—children would flock to him as he led singing and other activities at the ministry.

In many ways, Reggie was a carbon copy of Dolphus—outgoing, charismatic, handsome, and as touchy-feely as they come. Both are comfortable in the spotlight and know how to light up a crowd. But Reggie also had something in common with me: He loved being around elderly people. He could make them feel like a million bucks, and he enjoyed doing it. Back when Reggie was in elementary school, one of his teachers, Timothy Whitehead, periodically took the students out to pray with elderly residents in the community. One of the women they visited regularly called Reggie "my boy." She said she'd never seen a child pray like he did.

Though Reggie would later experience some ups and downs in his relationship with the Lord, I cherish the memory of him as a young person, encouraging our elderly neighbors through his prayers and his genuine care for them.

A Pleasant Surprise: Ryan

More than either of our older children, Ryan blends Dolphus's and my personalities. Like Dolphus, he is both athletic and an articulate speaker. When he was a very young child, we called Ryan "The Preacher" because he would set himself up behind a chair (to represent a pulpit) and chatter away, imitating his father's animated hand motions and delivery style. He hadn't actually learned to talk yet, so no one understood a word of Ryan's earliest messages, but that never seemed to trouble him.

An imaginative boy, Ryan also entertained himself for hours playing virtual video games. Not virtual reality games, but imaginary video games. He made all his own sound effects and imitated joystick use with his empty hands. While the other kids in his pre-school class napped (or tried to nap), Ryan would sit on his mat, enthusiastically playing his games. Dolphus eventually bought Ryan an actual video game, but I always enjoyed how creatively he invented his own.

After outgrowing these early exuberant activities, Ryan has resembled me a little more: shy and reserved, studious, and sometimes struggling to maintain self-confidence. We both have an unfortunate tendency to compare ourselves to others, and to find ourselves lacking.

Except when he's caught up in his music. Although he is good at many things, music is where Ryan really blossoms. We started him in a music class taught by a white woman down in Magee when he was only five or six years old. Unlike a lot of children, Ryan practiced his pieces diligently and became quite a good performer. He was in the band and choir at Genesis One, and he also sang in our church choir. In addition to music, Ryan got into computers in elementary school and discovered that he had talents in that area as well. Later on, he would combine these two interests, but I'm getting ahead of myself.

Ryan was in sixth grade when our family moved to Richland. He commuted to Genesis One for the remainder of that school year, and then we had to make a decision about what he would do for school. Lee Paris, the Chair of Mission Mississippi's Board and by now a good friend of Dolphus's, talked to us about Jackson Preparatory School. Ryan had already taken some art classes there, so it wouldn't be a completely unfamiliar environment, and there was no question he would get an excellent academic education, but Dolphus and I did have some reservations. Jackson Prep serves more than 500 students, and at that time, maybe six of those students were black. Dolphus told me about conversations he and Lee had about this fact.

"We just have to ask ourselves, 'Do we want our son to be subjected to being part of such a small minority in a predominantly white environment?'" Dolphus explained to Lee.

Lee countered by assuring Dolphus that Ryan would be treated well by both adults and students at the school. That was certainly nice to hear, but it didn't really answer our question, and Dolphus began to feel like his friend wasn't really hearing him. So he tried a different approach.

"Let's take everything Jackson Prep is," Dolphus suggested. "The great teachers, the excellent facilities, the assurance of a quality education. Now, paint all but a few of the faces black. Would you be comfortable sending your son there?"

A moment of silence followed, and Dolphus reported that Lee seemed to be getting a sense of what our concerns were. This is what Dolphus likes to call a "Mission Mississippi moment"—that point in a cross-cultural friendship when a person gets a new understanding of what someone else's experience has been like and comes to the realization that there is more than one perspective on any given situation.

We continued to think, talk and pray about the decision, and we finally made up our minds to send Ryan to Jackson Prep. We told him, though, that if he ever didn't want to be there, we would take him out.

Initially, Ryan took his ultra-minority status in stride better than the rest of the family did. He was the only black student in the band, and while Lee was right about his schoolmates being accepting of him, the band regularly traveled to different parts of the state to visit schools where there were no black faces, and where we didn't know how Ryan's presence would be received. I made it a point to go along to all of the away games.

Reggie had a lot of questions for Ryan about his experience at Prep, and the way he phrased those questions troubled Dolphus. "How did they treat you?" Reggie might ask Ryan when he arrived home from school. Or, "Did they speak to you? Did they do anything out of order?"

Dolphus took Reggie aside and told him, "Ryan's in the seventh grade. He's young and wide-eyed, and he's starting at a new school. Race isn't a big deal to him right now, but if we keep asking him 'they-questions,' it'll become a big deal. Let's not put our racial biases on him."

Reggie understood, and from then on he just checked in with Ryan now and then by asking how his day had gone.

Ryan did well at Prep—he got good grades, made the football and basketball teams, and enjoyed playing saxophone in the band. But eventually, the issue of race did come up. The thing that was hardest for Ryan was that some of the white students asked him questions about why black folks do this or that, or why they think a certain way.

"I'm just not comfortable answering for the whole black race," he eventually told Dolphus and me. He also explained that he felt bad if he gave one answer and then thought of a better one later. He started to feel like he wasn't smart enough to give the "right" answer the first time. (As if there could be a right answer to a question about how an entire race of people thinks about a given subject.) In short, he didn't like the pressure to represent his race, and we didn't blame him.

After eighth grade, Ryan left Prep and enrolled in Richland High School, where he flourished, despite a little bit of a rocky beginning. That first year, he played in the band, and he had fun teaching the other students new kinds of music and getting them to play pep songs at the games. The band director, however, was less than thrilled about the initiative Ryan had taken, and when that became evident, Ryan decided not to stay in the band.

He continued to pursue music less formally, writing his own raps and musical compositions, and making recordings of "beats" that he could sell to up-and-coming singing groups. He also played basketball for two years, served as the team manager after that, got involved in some student organizations, and won the school's Student of the Month award twice. And, despite his shyness, he became quite popular, and a lot of students began spending a lot of time at our house.

During the summers, Ryan acquired various types of work experience. While he was in middle school, he participated in a Boypreneur program at New Horizon Church in Jackson. The young men had to dress professionally (including neckties), and they went to classes at Jackson State and other local colleges to learn computer skills and study various other topics. The participants were divided into several teams, and each team had to plan and start its own small business (including drawing up business and marketing plans). One year, Ryan's group chose to sell zip-up neckties (a venture that may have begun with the desire to make their own lives easier…). Ryan won the Boypreneur of the Year award that summer.

For two summers, Ryan worked at Joanie Perkins Potter's law office. He loved that experience, and he enjoyed getting to know the Perkins family better after growing up with their legacy in Mendenhall. Though Dolphus and I hoped for a while that he might actually go into law, Ryan has since reminded us that as he doesn't much like reading, that's not a likely future for him.

When the time came for him to pick a college, Ryan faced a bit of a dilemma. Tougaloo College offered him a full scholarship, but he was reluctant to go there because it was where his older brother had gone. Belhaven University (then Belhaven College), which is known for its quality arts programs, offered him a partial scholarship. Ryan chose Belhaven and had a wonderful experience there. He enjoyed his classes, made a lot of friends, sang in the choir, took piano lessons, and even, to our surprise, appeared in some plays.

Belhaven is one of the most diverse Christian colleges in the country, and its President, Dr. Roger Parrott, has long been committed to racial reconciliation. Dolphus, who is a member of the University's Board of Trustees, was invited to speak on campus twice while Ryan was there, and he challenged the students to be intentional about pursuing reconciliation and building relationships across cultural differences. Ryan felt that the students really received that message, although he reports that dining hall seating continued to be largely self-segregated, as it is on so many college campuses. "I don't think it's intentional, really," he told me once. "The sports and dance groups are mixed, and they often eat together, but otherwise, I guess it's just easier for people to hang out with others of their own race."

Once he settled on a school, there was also the question of what major Ryan would choose. Initially, he wanted to major in music. Dolphus and I encouraged him to consider other options (that is to say, something more practical), and he eventually decided on (and completed) a communications major, with a music minor. Dr. Elayne Hayes-Anthony, the Chair of the Communications Department, has had a great influence on Ryan. Dr. Hayes-Anthony is an African-American woman from Braxton, Mississippi (just up the road from Mendenhall), and she has an excellent reputation on campus. During his junior year, Ryan heard about her from friends who were in her department. He met with her, decided to declare a communications major, and took all but one of the required courses the following year. (He was permitted to graduate with his class and took the final course he needed for his major that summer.)

Ryan's dream is to be a sound engineer (combining his musical talent with his technological savvy), and while he was still in school, he worked part-time at the John M. Perkins Foundation in inner-city Jackson, teaching music to kids and helping to set up a recording studio.

He has also interned at a local television station (one of the evening news anchors was an adjunct instructor at Belhaven) and worked at the State Capitol as a laptop technology assistant. The Capitol job was a session-only position, but his boss would have liked to keep Ryan on permanently, had budget cuts not made that impossible. As I write this, Ryan is looking for full-time work.

Like my own path, Ryan's road looks like it may wind a little bit, but that doesn't worry me too much. I feel certain that whatever he does for a living, his life will be spent honoring God by using the gifts of creativity, intelligence and kindness he's been given.

Chapter Eight
The Club No Parent Wants To Join: Losing our son, Reggie

I was flying to Dallas to meet Dolphus one time, and we ran into some horrible turbulence. A hurricane had just passed through the area, and I guess we caught the tail end of it. A couple of times, the plane just dropped through the air, and I was sure that we were going to crash, and I'd never see my family again. Dishes were flying about the cabin, people were being thrown around, and I clasped my hands and tried to think of all the things I wanted to say to my Maker before I went to meet Him.

As I sat there, praying fervently, I heard the voice of God. I know some people might not believe me when I say that, but no matter. I know what I heard. The voice said, "Look at your hands."

Look at my hands? Sometimes the things God says seem strange. But I looked.

"What do you see?"

The way I had clasped my hands, I could see the shape of a cross in them.

"There are going to be times in your life when you go through storms," the Lord told me. "It's going to get so rough, you may think you can't make it. When that happens, look to the cross; keep your eyes on me."

Then there was a loud noise, and the plane started falling. "Okay, Lord, I'm looking," I prayed, quickly. Suddenly, the pilot got control of the plane, things smoothed out, and sunlight began streaming through the windows. It was beautiful—for a few minutes.

Then the ride got bumpy again. And the voice spoke one more time. "This is the way life is sometimes."

We eventually landed safely in Dallas, though the flight took much longer than usual. Through the ups and downs of my life since then, I've remembered those moments on that plane when God assured me of His presence with and care for me, even during the worst of storms.

Reggie's life, in some ways, was like that flight— wracked by turbulence, but with brilliant bursts of sunshine in between. Sadly, neither the probable meningitis he had as a baby nor the lymphoma he battled as a child would prove to be the last of the storms Reggie faced.

As I mentioned before, for several years following his victory over cancer, Reggie thrived. He did well in school, participated in sports and other activities, and helped out with ministry programs. He was great in school and church plays— a talented actor, and very expressive. Everybody loved him and enjoyed being around him—he had an energy and a magnetism that were simply undeniable. (At times, Dolphus and I could have lived with a little less of the magnetism, as girls began calling our house at all hours of the day and night, but still, we appreciated Reggie's good nature and enthusiasm for life.)

During his teenage years, Reggie got into a few scrapes, as many young people do. He was never malicious, but sometimes his high spirits and mischievous nature just seemed to get the better of him. One time, Dolphus and I were going somewhere and realized we'd forgotten something at the house. When we returned, there was Reggie, driving off in the other car without our permission.

Another time, he did ask if he could borrow the car, but then instead of going to his friend's house, he and another boy drove over to the Junior High School to race each other.

Reggie ended up crashing into a transformer pole, totaling the car and seriously damaging the pole as well. Dolphus and I actually had to buy a replacement transformer pole—not something that was in our standard monthly budget.

For a while after that, Danita and Reggie took the bus to school, while Reggie worked to pay a portion of the damages. If it had been up to me, he would have paid the whole thing, but Dolphus is a little more lenient than I am. At the recommendation of the African-American police officer who responded to the accident, Reggie was also required to take a remedial driving course.

Two weeks before graduating, Reggie was expelled from high school. Fortunately, he had completed nearly all of the graduation requirements already. He enrolled in one correspondence course at the University of Southern Mississippi, and he received his diploma, although he wasn't able to march with his class at the commencement ceremony. Lillie Hardy (sister-in-law of Reggie's former Genesis One teacher, Marlene) was the coordinator of an annual community-sponsored Baccalaureate service. When she heard about Reggie's situation, she made sure he knew he was still welcome to participate in the Baccalaureate, which he did. A bright child who could get B's and C's in his classes without even studying, and higher marks when he put his mind to it, Reggie graduated from high school with academic honors despite the last-minute bump in the road.

He then enrolled at Tougaloo College. Like many college freshmen, he struggled at first to adjust to his new independence. In a report to the foundation that provided his scholarship, Reggie admitted, "I learned quickly that the responsibilities of me going to class and studying were no longer my parents urging me on but they were my responsibility." His grades dipped a bit that first semester, but he did significantly better in the spring—so much so that he was recognized as one of the most improved first-year students at the end of his second term. Later on, he would win a Spanish award, and Dolphus and I would come to campus for the ceremony at which he was honored. Another time, Dolphus spoke at the college. On both occasions, Reggie seemed happy to have us there, and he proudly introduced us to his friends.

And he had plenty of friends! As he had earlier in his life, Reggie continued to draw people to him. Although he never pledged a fraternity himself, he got to know many of the students in the "Greek" community, and he loved hanging out with his friends from the fraternities and sororities. He was a great dancer and always had fun going to parties and demonstrating his moves. Since some of his cousins were attending Jackson State University, on the other side of town, he spent a lot of time, and made a lot of friends, on that campus, as well. Reggie even charmed the ladies who worked in the dining hall. It might have been partly so he could sweet-talk them into giving him extra helpings of the food he liked, but I think it was mostly because he just loved people, and he made everyone he interacted with feel special.

Spiritually, as well as academically, Reggie worked to find his way during his first year at Tougaloo. For a while, he allowed his social life to crowd personal devotions and participation in a campus Bible study out of his schedule. But soon he realized that wasn't the way he wanted to go. He began to study the Word again, acknowledging both his need for Christ and his desire to serve God in his life.

Reggie didn't always take a full course load, so it took him five years to complete his college education. He graduated in 1999, with a major in Business Administration and a minor in Economics. He hoped to eventually own his own business, and also to help The Mendenhall Ministries with economic development efforts in the community.

After college, Reggie held a series of jobs, working for Mass Mutual, SunCom and finally Cellular South. Dolphus and I pushed Reggie into the Mass Mutual job because Dolphus knew someone at the company and thought working there would be a good opportunity for Reggie. As it turned out, Reggie didn't enjoy that job at all. He was never comfortable trying to convince people they wanted what he was selling. After a while, he made the decision to go after the job at SunCom, and I'm so glad he did. In a retail environment where people came to him already interested in the products and services he had to offer, he flourished. Reggie loved both of his telecommunications industry jobs, and a number of people told me over the years that they would drive past stores close to their homes so they could go to the one where he worked. They appreciated the kind of customer service he provided—how friendly and courteous he was to everyone, and how he would take the time to help his customers figure out exactly what phone plan or piece of equipment was going to be best for them.

In 2003, Reggie began dating a young woman named Michelle, whom Dolphus and I liked a lot. That was also the year Reggie and Dolphus attended a Promise Keepers conference in Jackson, and Reggie rededicated his life to Christ. Everything seemed to be going so well.

Our family has a New Year's Day tradition of sitting around the table together and talking about our hopes and dreams for the coming year. On January 1, 2004, Reggie told us he had some news. My first guess was that he and Michelle were engaged, and I remember thinking, as fond as I was of Michelle, that Reggie really wasn't ready to be married. Well, the news did involve Michelle, but they weren't engaged.

She was pregnant. That wasn't what we wanted to hear, and I feel bad now for how we responded to Reggie's announcement. Nobody expressed excitement for him, even though he was clearly happy about the coming baby.

Part of the reason for Reggie's joy was that, after his radiation and chemotherapy treatments, doctors had warned him that he would probably never be able to father a child. He was thrilled that they had been proved wrong.

Michelle felt she was too young to get married, but Reggie didn't let that dampen his spirits as he prepared for fatherhood. Each time they had a sonogram done, he would bring a copy to our house to put up on the fridge. He asked me to help him get food for Michelle that would be healthy for the baby. (His idea of what would be healthy for the baby occasionally missed the mark, but it was a very sweet effort, and I helped him out as much as I could.) After a month or two, as I got more used to the whole idea, I started asking questions about how Michelle was doing, and how things were going with the pregnancy. I still wasn't super happy about what was happening, and he probably knew that, but I tried to become more involved in this new and very significant season of my son's life.

Finances were a challenge for Reggie (he was making decent money, but he seemed to spend it just as quickly as it came in), so he moved in with us early that year. Dolphus worked with him on developing a budget, and soon Reggie had paid off most of his debts and started putting money into a savings account. Dolphus encouraged him to save $500 a month, so he would have room in his budget for rent when he moved into his own place. Reggie did that. In May, he and Dolphus began to look at possible houses for him to rent, but then Reggie decided that he'd prefer to buy. He wanted to have a home of his own to bring his new family into. Dolphus suggested that he wait a few months, so he could continue saving (now toward a down payment), and again Reggie agreed. So he continued to live with us.

At some point during these months, Reggie asked me if I would help with the baby after he or she was born. I assured him that I would do whatever I could to support him and his family. And I've kept this promise, though not at all in the way I expected.

On a Monday morning in June, Dolphus and I were getting ready to head to Baton Rouge for a couple of days for a conference. As Reggie was leaving for work that morning, I felt a sudden need to run after him and give him a hug. He was in the driveway, about to get in his car, when I caught up to him. We embraced, and then he said, "I love you, Mom."

Dolphus and I went on to the conference. I called Reggie a couple of times from Louisiana. One time he was able to talk; the other time, he had a customer, so I had to let him go.

We got home Wednesday evening. Reggie had left a shirt on our bed with a note wishing Dolphus a happy belated Father's Day. About 9:00 that night, he called to let us know he would be home soon. He also wanted to apologize to his dad for not celebrating with him the Sunday before. And he shared some ideas he had about a new phone he wanted me to get.

Dolphus and I were so tired from traveling, we went on to bed shortly after that. Before drifting off to sleep, I heard the front door open and slam. At the time, I thought it must have been Ryan getting home, because I was sure Reggie would have come in to see us if it was him.

Around 11:00 that night, the phone rang. It was the call every parent dreads. Dolphus answered, and the caller immediately started asking him questions, which he relayed to me.

Did we have a son named Reggie?

Did he have any distinguishing marks on his body?

He did. He had his name tattooed on his arm, and my name tattooed on his leg.

I fell on my face on the floor at the end of the bed and prayed. "God, whatever it is, please give me the strength; give me whatever I need to take it."

The caller wouldn't give Dolphus much information, just said there'd been an accident, and we should come to the hospital. So we threw on some clothes and rushed to the emergency room, leaving Ryan sleeping at home. Some police officers were waiting for us at the hospital, and they ushered us into a small room. That was when the doctors informed us that there had been a car wreck, and Reggie had been killed.

Later we pieced together what had happened. The slam of the door we had heard was Reggie coming home, but only to change clothes before going out again. Ryan, as it turned out, was already home, but he was watching television and didn't hear Reggie come in.

Earlier in the evening, Reggie had been hanging out with some friends and had been drinking fairly heavily (this was the first we knew of his being a binge drinker).

Apparently, when he left the house, his driving was erratic, and a police officer got behind him on Highway 49, near the I-20 interchange, and flashed his lights for Reggie to pull over. Instead of stopping, Reggie accelerated and led the officer on a high-speed chase along I-20, then north on I-55, all the way from Rankin County into Jackson. Finally, he exited the freeway at Northside Drive and pulled to the side of the road. According to police video, which Dolphus has watched, when the officer approached the window and said something to Reggie—probably instructing him to get out of the car—Reggie took off again. I'm sure he was terrified. He must have figured he'd be in big trouble, not only for the DUI, but also for the chase, and I guess he just panicked.

A few blocks down the road, Reggie swerved to miss hitting somebody, and he crashed into a tree. He wasn't wearing a seatbelt. The doctors said he died from head trauma—I never did find out if he died on the scene or later, at the hospital.

I do remember that he was still warm when they let us in to see him. And, to my surprise, there didn't seem to be a scratch on him—not that I could see, anyway. He just looked like he was sleeping peacefully. The police never found his billfold, but they gave Dolphus and me his clothes and other belongings.

Maybe because he looked asleep rather than dead, or maybe just because it's hard to comprehend such a terrible loss all at once, it didn't seem real to me at first. Even though we were doing all the things you do when somebody dies—including telling Danita and Ryan that their brother was gone—it still didn't seem real. I felt completely numb, like I was moving around, but not really functioning.

We went home and told Ryan first, and then a friend of Danita's, Marcus Turner, drove us down to Natchez to break the news to her. We pulled into her driveway and called to let her know we were there. She came to the door and immediately asked if something had happened to Reggie. She said she'd been having trouble sleeping all night. She'd been tossing and turning, and she had been praying for Reggie, because she was sure something was wrong with him.

When we told her what had happened, she immediately burst into tears. Dolphus and Ryan were crying, too. I was the only one who remained dry-eyed. I think maybe I was in shock. Once she'd calmed down a little, Danita said, "I knew Reggie was in trouble, I just didn't know it was that bad."

After we talked for a while, Danita got in the car with us, and we headed back to our house. It's about a two-hour drive from Natchez to Richland.

At a stop along the way, I confessed to Danita that I wasn't completely numb. I felt something. "I'm so mad at Reggie, I don't know what to do," I told her.

"I am, too," she said.

I was so angry, and so full of questions he'd never be able to answer. *Why were you drinking? Why did you drive when you were drunk? Why didn't you just stop and take your punishment?*

Occasionally, in the midst of the anger, there were moments of thankfulness that no one else had been hurt. At least we didn't have to live with the guilt and pain of other people dying because of something our child had done. Later we would find out how close Reggie had come to accidentally hurting another person. We received a letter from a gentleman—someone Dolphus had met through Mission Mississippi—who lived near the crash site. His daughter had been in their front yard when the accident happened. As this man put it, "Had Reggie's car veered to the right instead of to the left it would have come up onto my lawn and we might well be mourning the loss of two children." This brother in the Lord also told us how he had prayed for the driver of the car as paramedics did their work, even though he didn't know yet who the injured person was. So there were things to be grateful for.

But then I'd get mad all over again. There was a baby coming, and Reggie should be here to take care of his child. Kids are exposed to so much these days; they face so many challenges. They need their fathers. Reggie should be preparing to bring his child up in the Lord, and instead he was dead.

In my experience, the stages of grief are far from linear. They're not neat or orderly or predictable. I ricocheted from one to another to another and back again more times than I can count.

The morning after Reggie's death, as word got out, people began calling and coming by, and even with all these reminders that the accident really had happened, I slipped back into denial. Into that "going through the motions" mode of operations. I accepted the condolences, cards and food items. Dolphus and I talked through the arrangements that needed to be made. But I wasn't really there, and I didn't really believe it was happening.

I remembered Reggie "sleeping" at the hospital, and I just knew he'd be coming back. That's why I didn't put the chain on the door that night. I couldn't bear the idea of my son coming home and finding himself locked out.

It wasn't until my friends and colleagues, Bea Ross and Evelyn Njoroge, brought Dolphus and me a copy of the obituary to review that it finally hit me that Reggie was gone. I saw his sweet smiling face in the picture, and I just lost it. That was the first time I cried after his death, and once I started, I couldn't stop. I wept and wept, thinking about my special boy and all the life he would never live.

I thought about how Reggie had recently completed a "40 Days of Purpose" Bible study at church, and how he'd been looking forward to getting a house, and marrying Michelle, and raising their child. Even though he'd had his share of struggles and problems, it had seemed like he was making better choices. It had seemed like he had a bright future ahead of him. How could his life be over, just like that?

I knew without a doubt that Reggie was God's child, no matter what his problems had been (and even though he'd made some terrible decisions on the final night of his life), and that gave me some comfort. I remembered the times we'd almost lost him before, and I reminded myself that God had given us many more years with our special boy than had once seemed likely. I was grateful for each year—for each day— that we'd been given with Reggie. Still, the thought of putting him in the ground, of really having to say good-bye—it was almost more than I could bear.

Generally speaking, I'm not much of a crier. During my childhood, I watched my mother weep over difficult situations in her life, and at some point I decided I didn't want to live that way. So apart from occasional outbursts like the one I just described, I don't shed a lot of tears. Dolphus is much more outwardly emotional than I am, and he has a very tender heart, so he was the one who broke down more frequently after Reggie's death, and I did my best to comfort him. We embraced a lot during those early days, and we talked about what had happened and how we were handling it. I'm so grateful that in the wake of our loss, we didn't pull away from each other, as I know some couples do.

It seemed like the media folks were everywhere those first few days after Reggie's accident. We tried to avoid them, but every once in a while, Dolphus would say something to one of the reporters. I didn't talk to any of them. They were asking questions like, "How do you feel?" and I didn't have any idea how to answer that question, nor did I want to answer it.

As much as we were able, Dolphus and I tried to be there for Michelle and make sure she was okay. The morning after the accident, she saw the story on the news and called us to find out if it was really true. We had to tell her it was. She had a prenatal appointment later that day. It was the first one Reggie ever missed.

I didn't know how I would react when I first saw Reggie in his casket, at the funeral home. He had a peaceful expression on his face, along with a sly smile. He looked so much like himself, and so relaxed, that I actually started to feel a little better. Of course, it was incredibly difficult to see him lying there lifeless, but I think it would have been even harder if he'd looked like he was in pain.

I turned to Danita, and I said, "He's okay."

Reggie's wake was held on a Monday night. It had been so hard for us to prepare for this moment that we were late getting there. The place was packed when we arrived; there were so many people that they had overflowed the sanctuary and spilled out into the foyer. Pastor Neddie Winters was emceeing the program, and he invited people to greet us when we got there. As our friends and neighbors hugged us and offered their words of condolence and encouragement, we were overwhelmed, not only by how many had come, but by the great distances some of them had traveled to stand with us in our time of mourning.

The service itself was a very special time. Our church choir sang, a young man named Darryl Smith sang a beautiful song as well, and Vera Mae Perkins led us in a round of "My Lord Knows the Way through the Wilderness." A PowerPoint slide show, with some of Reggie's favorite Gospel music in the background, showed photos of him as a baby and on through the years. People were given an opportunity to share, and many people from different stages of his life spoke about the impact Reggie had had on them. Dr. Tree and Betty Gentry, two of the medical professionals who had treated him during his bout with cancer, spoke. John Perkins shared. Vince Gordon, a local Young Life leader, gave a brief message. It was amazing to see how many people Reggie had touched in his short life. Everyone remembered what a dynamic, uplifting presence he had been, and how he had brightened things up just by walking into the room. As one friend of ours expressed it, "He brought with him a ray of sunshine—no matter his inner feelings or circumstances." There was great comfort in being among people who loved us; loved Reggie; and spoke such kind, grateful and affirming words about our son.

Then it was Tuesday. Once again, I felt like I was outside my own body—like this couldn't really be happening to me. Some friends from Arkansas, Shelby and Ruth Smith, came by and visited us that morning. So did Dolphus's sisters, Kathy Large and Elgia Clayton. They brought breakfast from Shoney's and sat with us for a while.

Getting ready to bury Reggie was impossibly hard. Danita and I both struggled even to get dressed, knowing what it was we were preparing for. The limousine arrived, and we still weren't ready. The driver had to wait.

Because the funeral was held during the week, and since so many people had come out for the wake, we didn't expect many people to be able to make the service. We were shocked when the limousine pulled up to the funeral home, and we saw cars parked all up and down the street. From the funeral home, we drove as a group to Mendenhall Bible Church, where the service would be held, and where even more people were waiting.

A pastor from California; people who served with Dolphus on the Boards of World Vision, InterVarsity Christian Fellowship, and the Evangelical Council for Financial Accountability; a couple of mayors; plus countless extended family members, friends and neighbors were there. We didn't want the day to be about who came, so we decided not to introduce the dignitaries during the service. As I looked over the crowd, though, I thanked God that so many people loved us and cared about what we were going through. Their presence was a precious gift that helped me get through that excruciating day.

The service began, and once again we were blessed by the time we spent remembering and celebrating Reggie. The choir from Voice of Calvary Fellowship in Jackson sang, as did Minnie Holloway, a long-time friend with a beautiful, powerful voice. Many of Reggie's schoolmates were there, and several of them shared about the impact his life and death had made on them.

I felt that it was important for Dolphus and me to bear witness, even during this most difficult time, to God's grace and love. I absolutely believed (and still do believe) that He can and does help us in our worst pain. His power is able to take us through our trials, even though we cry, and even when it's so hard we think we can't possibly make it. God honored the prayer I had uttered while lying face-down on the floor that first night. He gave me the strength to get up and worship him in the midst of Reggie's homegoing service. I couldn't have done that on my own.

We buried Reggie in the Mendenhall Bible Church cemetery. People had sent so many flowers, we placed some of them on other graves. Then it was over, but we weren't ready to be alone, so Dolphus invited some friends and family members over to our house. We talked and visited for a while, but eventually they all had to leave.

And that's when it was really, really real. All the things we'd had to do were done. The people had come and gone. They had been wonderful—they'd helped us get through the family hour and the funeral—but now they were gone. Now it was quiet. And there we were, with one empty place at the table and time to think. That was a hard moment.

Sometimes I feel like I should apologize to all the people I know who lost children before Dolphus and I did. I always knew they were going through something awful, and I tried to be there for them, but I didn't really understand. It's hard to lose anyone you love, but it's different with a child. It's a different kind of pain, because your children are part of you. My sister, Esta, is one of the people I have apologized to. Six years before we lost Reggie, Esta's daughter, Chasity, and Chasity's two young children were killed in their home. Even now, I don't have the words to describe how terrible and devastating this tragedy was. But I do have a better understanding of the pain my sister has been living with since that awful day.

When you lose a child, you join a club of sorts. It's not a club anyone wants to join, and membership in this club is not something you would ever wish on anyone else, and yet, once you're in it, you're so grateful for the other people who are in it, too. The people who helped Dolphus and me the most after Reggie's death were other parents who had lost children. When we shared our story through a *Daily Guideposts* article, we began getting letters from people who had experienced similar losses. These kind, heartfelt notes encouraged us so much that we now try to reach out, even to people we don't know, or don't know well, whenever we hear of someone losing a child.

I remember a preacher who came by to visit Dolphus and me after Reggie's death. This man had lost a daughter to suicide. He had a simple question for us: "Have you had a good holler yet?" When he said that, I thought about the day John and Vera Mae Perkins's oldest son, Spencer, died of a heart attack. That evening, I'd heard Mrs. Perkins's anguished screams. Of course, even then I had understood that she and her family were going through a terrible storm, and that they were in great pain. But now I can identify with that scream. I understand the helplessness, frustration and agony you feel in that moment when you realize your child is never coming back.

That's not to say, of course, that you can't encourage or comfort someone who's grieving just because you haven't gone through the exact same thing. Some people stay away from folks who are mourning because they're worried they don't know the right thing to say, and that's unfortunate. More than the perfect words, it's the presence of someone who cares that matters. You can be quiet, or you can talk about other things—and sometimes that's better. It's almost always better than spouting platitudes, or offering unsolicited advice, or running down a list of the dead person's faults, or some of the other things people do when they're not sure what to say.

I remember when one of the pastors in TMM's Pastors Development Group died suddenly. His wife was having a really hard time, so several of the other wives from the group decided to visit her. We brought food, and paper products so she wouldn't have to clean up, and we all sat around the table, eating and talking. We weren't really sure what the best thing to do was, but we jumped in and trusted we'd find our way. We began reminiscing, and soon we got to laughing and talking about all sorts of other things. As we got ready to leave, the widow's mother thanked us over and over again. "This is the first time she's laughed," she told us. We were able to let our friend know we cared and were there for her without dwelling on what had happened.

Sometimes the best thing is to send a note or a card. Something simple, just to let people know you love them and are praying for them. Dolphus and I cherished the many kind notes we received in the days, weeks, even months after Reggie's death. It's such a comfort to be reminded that you are not alone, and that people care about your pain, and about you.

A few days after Reggie's funeral, Dolphus and I invited the Mission Mississippi staff over to our house. It wasn't a fancy affair—we just picked up some food from KFC and ate lunch together. We wanted to thank Dolphus's co-workers for being so fantastically supportive during the tragedy we had experienced. We didn't expect or want these friends to come to the table with profound words of wisdom or the answers to all of our questions. We just wanted them to join us at the table, to be our friends and co-laborers, as they had been for so many years. As we had with the pastor's wife, we talked about all sorts of things besides Reggie's death, and we laughed together. That was a precious time.

The REAL Christian Foundation staff and volunteers (Linda Jackson, Evelyn Njoroge, Bea Ross) were amazing, too. People from our church, people from the community—so many people reached out to us and held us up with their love.

Dolphus and I are firm believers in counseling, so in addition to the support we received from family and friends, we also sought professional help in dealing with our loss. I'm very glad we did that, for a couple of reasons. For one thing, it helped each of us to be able to talk through what we were thinking and feeling along the way. When you've never been through something before, you don't really know what's normal. You're not sure what's "okay." Some days you'll feel better, and then the next thing you know, you're crying again, and you don't know why. Some days I had real trouble thinking; I just couldn't seem to get my mind moving or keep it on track, and I worried that I might be going crazy. It's encouraging to have someone you trust who can say, "You don't have to be worried about that. That's just part of the grieving process."

The other important thing about the counseling was that it helped Dolphus and me understand and respect each other's processes. A lot of marriages break up after a child's death, and I suspect a major contributor to that is that often people don't talk about what's going on, and they don't understand the different way their partner is grieving the loss.

One person might be crying a lot, and the other isn't, so the first person thinks he or she is the only one grieving. One person might need some space, and the other one takes that as a rejection.

Our counselor helped Dolphus and me to see that it was okay for us to grieve differently. It didn't mean that either of us loved Reggie less, or that we were doing anything wrong. We learned that we might not always be ready to talk about something at the same time, but that if one person wanted to talk, the other could at least listen. We learned that there are a whole lot of "normal" things to feel and do as part of a grieving process, and we were able to give each other permission to move forward in our own ways.

Mrs. Perkins also shared some wisdom with us from her own experience. She and Rev. Perkins had grieved Spencer's death very differently. While Mrs. Perkins withdrew and stayed in bed for long stretches of time, Rev. Perkins seemed to cope with his pain by redoubling his ministry efforts. He resumed his traveling schedule a couple of weeks after Spencer's death, and that was hard for Mrs. Perkins. So she admonished Dolphus to stay close to me as we began to work through our loss.

We took what she said to heart, even though in some ways, she and Dolphus grieved more similarly than she and I did. We decided that, as much as possible, I would go with Dolphus when he traveled. I wanted to be near my husband as we worked our way through the grieving and healing processes; I didn't ever want either of us to feel like we'd been left alone in our pain.

Six years later, we're still muddling through. It's still hard. But we're making it. And we're growing.

Immediately after Reggie's death, I got really paranoid. I was so afraid something would happen to Danita or Ryan, too. It was hard not to be over-protective of them. I had to learn how to trust God with my children, knowing that His promise of faithfulness didn't necessarily mean they would be protected from harm. It's a different kind of trust—not believing that God will do what I want Him to do, but believing that He will be with me through whatever happens.

One day, I went up to the Medical Mall in Jackson for a doctor's appointment, and on the way I started having my own little pity party. "Why?" I asked God. "Why, when some people have car wrecks and walk away just fine, did our child have to die?" As I pulled into the lot and parked my car, a song about God's sovereignty came on the radio. And it felt like God had sent that song across the airwaves just for me. "The Lord my God is sovereign. He can do whatever He wants to do," the singer proclaimed. A few moments later, "Who am I to question His wisdom?" I remembered those other parents in the pediatric cancer ward, and how I'd realized it was wrong to ask, "Why me?" as if I should be exempt from suffering when other people aren't. I started crying. "God, I'm sorry. Please forgive me," I prayed.

Our shared loss has also strengthened the ties among Dolphus, Danita, Ryan and me. We've always been close as a family, but we have a greater sense now that time is short, and we should make the most of it while we're together. We spend more time talking, and really listening to each other. We do more things together—including vacations, which we rarely made time for before Reggie died.

For a while, Dolphus and I wrestled with the feeling that we were being disloyal to Reggie if we did things for Ryan that we hadn't done for him. We had to consciously recognize that Reggie was gone, but Ryan was still here, and we were Ryan's parents. Our job was to do what we needed to do for Ryan, not try to measure our affection and provision, as if this were a competition between our two boys.

There are some things I regret about how we raised Reggie. Mostly I wish we'd given him more freedom to be himself and chart his own course in life. We struggled, sometimes, to trust Reggie to make wise decisions, and I think we tried to be the voice of the Holy Spirit in his life—which I guess means we also struggled to trust God. We didn't intentionally try to usurp His place, of course, but we sometimes strongly encouraged Reggie to do what we thought would be best for him, rather than get out of the way and allow God to guide Reggie into the opportunities and situations that He knew were best. We loved our son dearly, and I don't think he ever doubted that, but we probably put some unrealistic expectations and unnecessary pressure on him, and I'm sure that was hard for him.

Yes, there are definitely some things I would do differently if I could do it again.

And in a way, God has given Dolphus and me that opportunity.

Two months after Reggie's death, again at 11:00 at night, our phone rang. This time it was Michelle, calling to tell us her baby had just been born. I went to the hospital the next morning to meet her son, whom she named Reggie, after his father. Dolphus and I call him Li'l Reggie.

Li'l Reggie is like a clone of our Reggie. He's outgoing, playful, funny, loving and very affectionate, though he does have a bit of a stubborn streak. He has brought tremendous light and joy back into our lives. He calls us

Grandma and Pops, and Michelle graciously allows us to see him whenever we want. Li'l Reggie loves coming over to our house, going to the park, reading, watching videos, and talking about Jesus. When we eat together, he wants to be the one to say the blessing.

He's an intelligent and articulate child, using words that are above his grade-level (like "invisible," "awesome," and "extraordinary," to name just a few) and demonstrating excellent reasoning skills. He loves to talk in Spanish, which he's learning in kindergarten, and he thinks spelling "Mississippi" is great fun. Like his father and grandfather, he's comfortable being the center of attention, he enjoys traveling, and he loves meeting new people.

Also like his dad and granddad, Li'l Reggie already has a keen eye for racial dynamics. We recently took a trip to a Chicago suburb, and a friend of ours there took us to the local zoo. At one point, Li'l Reggie looked around and said, "Grandma, it's only white folks here!" We hope and trust that as he grows, Li'l Reggie will not only continue to be observant of the environment around him, but that he'll also become a bridge-builder in his own right, reaching out in friendship to people from different backgrounds and cultures.

And, like our Reggie before him, Li'l Reggie is a trickster. One Sunday, Li'l Reggie and I, along with some guests who were staying at our home at the time, accompanied Dolphus to a guest preaching engagement at a church in Jackson. I was working at the book table, so when Li'l Reggie needed to use the restroom, one of our friends agreed to take him. Li'l Reggie refused to go into the ladies' room with her, so she waited in the hallway while he went into the men's room. Soon, she heard him yelling, "Miss Jodie! Miss Jodie, I'm stuck in here!" Jodie dashed into the men's room and immediately got down on the floor to crawl into the stall and let Li'l Reggie out. As she did so, he unlocked the door and exclaimed, "Gotcha!" Fortunately, no men walked into the room while our friend was crawling on the floor!

I think it's probably fair to say that I'm the person in the family most likely to be stern with Li'l Reggie when his behavior becomes a little too rambunctious, so he and I do have our run-ins from time to time. I remember one occasion, when Li'l Reggie was about four, and we were driving in the car. I'd scolded him about something, and he announced his intention to exchange me for a more lenient model: "I'm gonna go to the Grandma store and buy another Grandma," he informed me.

"Is that right?"

"Yes."

"And this new Grandma of yours, do you think she'll pick you up from school every day? Will she take you to the store to buy tennis shoes, and to karate class and swimming lessons, and to Chuck E. Cheese and GattiTown?"

Li'l Reggie considered all this for a few moments, and then the verdict came back: "Okay, I'll keep you."

We talk to Li'l Reggie about his father quite a bit. We still have the sonograms on our refrigerator door, and we tell him how his Daddy was so happy and proud about the baby growing in Mommy's tummy. Li'l Reggie knows which room in the house belonged to our Reggie, and he likes to play there. I think he feels close to his father when he's in that place.

Michelle is very much a part of our lives as well. She calls us Mom and Pops, and we do our best to be there for her and give her advice from time to time. We've gotten to know members of her family and have become friends with them. We enjoy Li'l Reggie together.

Of course, none of this "makes up" for losing Reggie, but all of it reminds me that God really does have an amazing way of bringing good things out of even the worst and most painful experiences of our lives.

After Reggie's death, we found a prayer he had written and saved on his computer. "Thank you for working on me," he had told God. "Thank you for the valley low I've been in. Thank you for the mountains to climb and for climbing gear you are providing me." It gives me profound joy to know that my son, even at a relatively young age, had the spiritual maturity to appreciate the value of challenges he'd faced in his life. I'm so glad he knew God was with him—in the valleys, on the mountaintops, and for all the steps in between. I remind myself of this truth as I continue in my own walk with God, enduring and learning from the lows, celebrating the highs, and always looking to Him for the strength to keep climbing.

Chapter Nine
On Speaking: The difficulty of making words come out, in public and in private

I still remember my first public speaking disaster like it was yesterday. I was about eight years old, maybe ten, and Easter was coming up. At our church, we had programs for all the holidays: Christmas, Easter, Mother's and Father's Days. Various children and youth from the congregation would recite poems to honor the occasion.

Many kids simply read the poems they had chosen, but I was a perfectionist, even then, so I memorized mine. My mother helped me learn it, and I practiced saying the poem over and over and over, until I knew it so well I couldn't possibly forget any part of it.

I didn't even bring a written copy with me when it was my turn. I knew that poem backwards and forwards.

And then I looked out into the crowd—all those people watching me and waiting to hear what was going to come out of my mouth.

Nothing did.

I could not think of the opening line of the poem for anything. It was one of those moments that probably only lasted a few seconds, but felt like an eternity.

There were two memorable responses from audience members.

On one side sat my father, smiling and trying to encourage me. "It's okay, take your time," I heard him say.

But on the other side of the room, some girls started giggling, and my confidence plummeted.

Even though I recovered and said my poem, the image that stuck with me was those girls laughing at me. I've struggled with public speaking ever since.

They say "the devil's in the details," and while this may not be exactly how that phrase is generally interpreted, it sure does seem to me that Satan is awfully effective at using little things to try to keep people from being all that God created us to be.

I remember my father's loving, affirming, supportive words and facial expression from that day. I do. But when I get up to speak in front of a group, the voice in my head echoes those girls. It taunts me, mocks me, and tells me I'm a failure before I've even gotten started. For 50 years, those few seconds of my stage fright and their ridicule have haunted me.

Fortunately, I don't get asked to speak very often (that's one of the great things about being married to Dolphus—he's the speaker in the family), but occasionally I do, and it's always something of an ordeal for me. Dolphus says I do too much planning, and maybe he's right, but I can't imagine approaching a microphone *without* extensive preparation. I spend hours praying and making notes, trying to get my ideas organized and presentable.

Even after all that preparation, and with my notes right in front of me, I tend to ramble when I get nervous. So I take longer than I'm supposed to, without actually saying that much. My voice breaks, I trip over words, and sometimes my mind goes completely blank.

That happened when I was speaking to a group in Gulfport one time. I lost my train of thought, I couldn't find my place in my notes, and I just had no idea what to say. It was so awful, I actually started crying. One of the event organizers came onstage and prayed for me, but I just couldn't do it. I could not speak.

As miserable and humiliating as public speaking meltdowns can be, a larger problem for me has actually been my struggle with private speaking. Like my mother, I've generally preferred not to rock any boat that's upright, even if I can see that it has other problems. But a slow leak can eventually cause at least as much trouble as a sudden shift in balance might.

After decades of keeping things inside, I finally realized that I was killing my own spirit, a little bit at a time. On the surface, Dolphus seemed to be faring better. As far as I could tell, after every disagreement we had, he would move on and be fine, while I kept my resentment, my hurt feelings, and all the things I hadn't said bottled up in my own mind. But it can't have been fun for him, either, having a wife who was often moping or giving him the silent treatment.

In 1997, the same year we left The Mendenhall Ministries, Dolphus and I started seeing a counselor. Sometimes we went together; sometimes I went alone. I knew that in order to feel complete, I needed to start speaking up for myself.

But that was kind of a daunting prospect. In addition to my own issues with speaking and self-esteem, I had to deal with a fact of Dolphus's nature: He can be a little bit intimidating! He's articulate, he's strong-willed, and he has one of those personalities that can loom larger than life sometimes. I felt a little bit like a novice skier who had decided to bypass the bunny slopes and go straight to the black diamond runs.

But the counseling was helping me realize that the things I had to say mattered. They were important. It was worth making the effort to say them, even if that was scary.

So I tried. And the world didn't end. Sure, it was kind of unsettling for both Dolphus and me at first. We'd gotten used to one way of relating, and now here was something very different. But we were both committed to the process, and over time it's gotten easier.

Once again, it's the little things that I look to for signs of growth. It used to be, if Dolphus used a tone of voice that irked me, I wouldn't say anything to him about it, but my annoyance would grow completely out of proportion over the following hours or days. I've learned to just stop and say, "Wait a minute. What did you mean by that?" And maybe he was being rude and needs to apologize, or maybe I misinterpreted what he was saying. Either way, in two minutes the whole thing is sorted out, and we can move on. It's amazing how much time, energy and emotion you can save by nipping something in the bud!

As I practiced expressing my opinion more often, I had to learn some things about offering constructive criticism. Early on, I tended to focus on the negative. For instance, Dolphus might have chosen a tie that didn't go well with the shirt he was wearing. So I would tell him, "Honey, that tie's gotta go."

That would immediately shut him down. "Fine, you choose one," he might say.

Eventually, I learned that a more helpful approach was to offer a positive alternative from the outset. "Why don't you try this tie?" I might suggest. "I think it would look really nice with that outfit."

Again, this is a small example, but it was an important lesson for me. Being willing to express myself was great, but I needed to be careful about how I did so. Because most people, not just Dolphus, don't respond well to criticism that feels like an attack. And whether or not I achieved the desired outcome (in my example, Dolphus changed his tie either way), our relationship would be in much better shape if I approached him, not as the fashion police, but as a partner who wanted the best for him (or, in this case, for his outfit).

Especially as we moved into a season of our life together, with the founding of REAL Christian Foundation, where we were going to function more as partners and less as boss/employee, I needed to grow into that role in a way that would be good for both of us. And I think I have. Dolphus and I don't yell at each other, but we do feel free to disagree, and to talk through those disagreements when they arise. I'm still not as articulate as Dolphus is, but I don't let that stop me any more. I say what I feel needs to be said, and he listens. And, of course, I still listen to him, too.

Listening is something I've always been good at—I'd even venture to say it's a gift God has given me. Throughout my years at TMM, that was always something I felt I had to offer—not only to people who were using the ministry's services, but to my co-workers as well. One woman has always called me her "psychologist" because she knows I'm willing to listen to her talk about the things that are going on with her—problems, decisions she needs to make, whatever. And even if I don't have any brilliant advice to offer her (and most of the time, I don't), she says she knows she'll be okay if she can just talk things through with me.

Another former colleague and dear friend, Bea Ross, has also told me how much she depends on my listening to her. Bea is an amazing woman. She's heavily involved in the work of her church, and she's an excellent speaker. Very articulate. She also has an incredible memory and is quite personable and caring. She worked with us at TMM for years, and she was always great at developing and maintaining friendships with volunteers who came to serve with the ministry. Now that we no longer work together, we don't talk as often, but whenever we do, we get going and have trouble stopping. Eventually, one or the other of us will realize how long we've been on the phone. It means the world to me that someone so talented relies on my listening ear.

So even though listening isn't a skill that is valued publicly the way speaking is, I'm glad God has given me the ability, as well as the inclination, to really hear other people when they need to talk.

I haven't asked them, but I think our children have appreciated the "new me" as I've emerged over the last decade or so. My tendency, earlier on, to start sentences with the words, "But your father says..." perpetuated for them a culture in which only one person really had a say. At least, the boys mostly followed the example I set.

Danita, despite her many similarities to me, never had trouble speaking up for herself.

I remember many occasions on which Dolphus had made plans for the whole family to do something or other. Now, Dolphus has amazing reservoirs of energy, and he can be something like a force of nature when he gets going. For years, Reggie, Ryan and I would simply allow ourselves to be swept up by that force and carried off to whatever it was Dolphus wanted us to do. Danita, though, would calmly consider whether or not she wanted to go along (this was once she was old enough to exercise an independent choice about these things, of course).

"You know what, Dad? I'm pretty tired. I think I'm just going to stay home," she'd say every once in a while.

I still remember the liberation I felt, realizing that I could say, "I'm going to sit this one out, too."

I hope I haven't painted Dolphus as a tyrant. He isn't. He's a wonderful, godly man. But we did establish some patterns early on in our marriage that we eventually realized needed to change. And change is almost always hard, even if everyone involved agrees it's the right thing to do. So we've worked at it, we've struggled from time to time, and we've grown together.

We've each become better people as we wrestled with these issues, and our relationship has become closer. So even the struggle has been a gift, in its own way.

Now that you've read all of this, you can probably more fully understand how hesitant I was when various people (Dolphus, the Board of REAL Christian Foundation, and a few others) first suggested that I tell my story in a book. On the positive side, at least I wouldn't have to memorize anything, and if the words didn't come out right the first time, we could always fix them later.

Still, I resisted the idea for a long time. Because it isn't just the getting up in front of people and opening my mouth part of speaking that has been hard for me over the years. It's also the part where I have to believe I have something worth saying.

To be honest, I'm still not completely convinced that I do. Except in the sense that we all have something worth saying. Throughout Scripture, God's people are instructed to tell the stories of how God has worked in their lives in the past. God has worked in my life. My hope is that as I speak of the things He has done, the story has value to those who hear it.

Dolphus and the folks he works with at Mission Mississippi talk about this a lot. They talk about how helpful it is, when pursuing reconciliation, for people to tell their stories to one another (and to listen to each other's stories). Some of us are naturally better at telling, and some are better at listening, but I believe we all grow and benefit as we share, and seek to understand, the experiences that have made us who we are.

So I appreciate the people who have encouraged me to tell my story, and I deeply appreciate each person who has taken the time to read it. You honor me with your willingness to listen.

Chapter Ten
Being Rosie: Thoughts about identity, ministry and the future

"You are so lucky to be married to Dolphus Weary!"

Time and time again, people approach me after hearing Dolphus speak, and they say those words to me.

I usually just smile and say, "Thank you," or, if I'm in a feisty mood, I might comment, "Yes, we're blessed to have each other."

But I have to confess, sometimes I bristle at the implication (unintentional, I'm sure) that I don't deserve to be Dolphus's wife. On occasion, I have to fight the urge to say, "You know, he didn't do so badly himself."

Earlier in our married life, I worried about people thinking Dolphus had married down. In terms of career, charisma, and so forth, I was afraid they would think he could have done better. And there probably are people out there who think that. I don't worry about them so much any more, though, because after 40 years of marriage, Dolphus and I both recognize the things of value and substance that each of us has brought to the table. In fact, I can laugh about it now, and he and I sometimes laugh about it together. "They think I'm the lucky one, but we know the truth, don't we?" I might tease him.

But I'm just teasing, because there is real truth in what people say to me—I am lucky (or fortunate, or blessed, whichever term you prefer) to be married to Dolphus Weary. When I think about all the ways life could have turned out for a shy, poor, African-American girl from Mississippi, I am profoundly grateful for Dolphus and the relationship we have, not only as husband and wife, but also as parents, grandparents and co-laborers for the gospel. The life we've built together has been incredibly rich and rewarding, and the opportunity to share that life with Dolphus has been one of God's greatest gifts to me.

I've learned many things from Dolphus. One of the most valuable lessons he's taught me is to meet challenges head-on. My tendency is to fear the unknown and back away from tasks or steps that look difficult. But Dolphus pushes me to do the very things I'm most afraid to do. He reminds me that the more I do those things, the better I'll become at doing them. He tells me I can do anything I want to do.

Dolphus also reminds me, over and over again, that I am special in God's sight—and also in his. He assures me that the only person I need to be is myself—that it's enough for me simply to be Rosie Camper Weary, a woman God has made to reflect His image.

Which brings us to another (internal) response I often have when people compliment me on being Dolphus's wife. I never want to just be that. I don't want to be defined solely by who my husband is. Yes, I am Mrs. Dolphus Weary—and happily so. But I am also Rosie.

In many ways, I have spent much of my adult life in Dolphus's shadow. I have sometimes lived vicariously through him. As I think about the future—about what's still ahead for me to do and be—I know I'm going to keep striving to find the right balance between being one with my husband and being my own person.

What's really wonderful is that Dolphus, far from trying to keep me in his shadow or behind him in any way, is the one encouraging me to stretch my own wings and fly. He's the one who has been pushing me to tell my story. And he's been helping me see the value of the behind-the-scenes contributions I've made to our ministry over the years. I thank and praise God for giving me a husband who loves me, affirms me, and encourages me to be everything God wants me to be—whatever that is.

And I do still long to find my own niche, to discover that thing that I truly love to do, and that I'm uniquely gifted to do. I've tried my hand at many different kinds of work over the years, and I don't consider those efforts wasted. I am thrilled to have had the opportunity to spend 39 years in ministry, and I'm grateful that God has used me in many ways during that time. But I would love to spend a season of my life feeling like I am doing what I was created to do, and that I am really making a difference in the world. I don't know yet what that thing might be, but I am certain that as I continue to think and pray about this question, Dolphus will support me and help me find my way.

In this book, I've talked a lot about struggles: my own internal battles with low self-confidence and depression, the external problems of poverty and racism, tragic losses of loved ones, and challenges in personal and professional relationships. My purpose in sharing about these struggles is not to blame anyone for the things in my life that have been difficult, or to make you think poorly of anyone (myself or others I've written about). My purpose is simply to tell my story the way I understand it. More than that, it's to tell the story of God's liberating power working in my life, with the hope that others who face struggles and challenges in their own lives will be strengthened in their belief that God can and will bring them through the hard parts. And that as He sustains and heals them, He will also prepare them for whatever new season they will enter beyond their present trials.

It's 2010 as I write this, and this feels like an appropriate time to be thinking about new possibilities for the future. Less than two years ago, our country elected our first African-American President. I remember those primary elections, when Illinois Senator Barack Obama kept winning, and many of us found hope and doubt waging war in our hearts.

As we followed the news closely, listening to everything we could and waiting to see how the election would play out, I remembered an incident many years earlier, when Rev. Jesse Jackson was running for President. Some white Republican friends of ours had invited Dolphus and me to spend time with them at their cabin out west. One night while we were there, Rev. Jackson was scheduled to make a televised speech. Dolphus and I wanted to hear what he had to say. Our friends did not. They stayed out on the porch while we watched the broadcast, and they were upset with us for even wanting to listen to the speech.

One of the wonderful things about then-Senator Obama's campaign was that it was clear he would be a President for the people, not just for black people. And many Whites supported him—not grudgingly, but with great enthusiasm. They recognized that he was qualified to fill the position of President. You often hear people say, "I'd love to hire a black person for this job, but I can't find anyone who's qualified," and sometimes that's probably true, and sometimes it's probably an excuse. With Senator Obama, many people who didn't agree with his politics, and who had no intention of voting for him, at least acknowledged that he was qualified to compete for the office.

I'll never forget the day he was elected. It was the greatest feeling in the world, seeing how far our country has come. I've always been proud to be an American, but on that day, I was truly elated.

This isn't to say that I agree with all of President Obama's politics. But I'm thankful for this sign of our nation's growth and progress, and I pray frequently for our current President, as I prayed for previous Presidents with whose politics I didn't always agree.

I pray for Michelle Obama, too. Talk about a shadow a wife could get lost in! But she seems to be holding her own. She comes across as a genuine class act—a woman who is able to be herself in the spotlight—and I'm delighted that she serves as a role model, not just for her own daughters, but for so many other young girls growing up in these rapidly changing times.

As I think back to my own childhood, and how few avenues seemed to be open to black women, and to Blacks in general, I'm delighted that African-American and other minority children today can look to the Obama family and believe that anything is possible. I pray for the young people who participate in programs at The Mendenhall Ministries and the rural ministries we support through REAL Christian

Foundation, that they will feel free to dream big dreams about their futures. I pray that they will learn to step out in faith and see where God leads them, and how He provides for them and opens doors they never expected to walk through.

I also pray for people who are in ministry, or going into ministry, in communities where it's still hard for children (or adults for that matter) to imagine a bright future. Dolphus and I know from our own experience how exhausting and often discouraging it is to labor for change and growth when circumstances seem to be aligned against you, and people's hopes have been dashed over and over again.

Generally, I prefer not to give advice. As I've said before, I'm better at listening to and encouraging people as they think through situations and decisions in their lives. That said, there are some things I've learned during our years in ministry that I'd like to offer to others laboring in (or thinking about laboring in) the "trenches" of community development-type ministry.

First, I would say that it's important to remember whose ministry it is. It's God's work, not yours or mine. So often, we try to do things on our own. Then, if our efforts fail, we blame God. What we need to do is trust God to do ministry through us. We need to see ourselves as His ambassadors, and as His laborers, rather than as the owners of the work. This perspective will make it easier (I might even say, possible) to weather the inevitable ups and downs of a life in ministry.

Which brings us to another point: It's important to recognize that there are going to be difficulties. Some people have a romanticized view of ministry—trust me, it's not all roses or warm, fuzzy moments. There will be setbacks, failures and disappointments.

So it's essential, especially if you're a couple going into ministry together, to pray, think and talk about what you're getting ready to do. Make sure you have a reasonably accurate understanding of what it is you're getting into, and that you and your spouse have similar understandings of what it is you're getting into. Of course, there will be surprises. Things won't go as you expected, and you'll have to adjust course midstream. Still, I think it's important to take some time, before you jump in, to consider what it is you're committing to. And to earnestly seek guidance from God about whether this is something He has for you. If you feel in your spirit that He is calling you to the work, you'll be able to return to that conviction when the road gets bumpy.

And don't just pray before you get started. Pray with your spouse, if you have one, and/or with other ministry partners on a regular basis. Constantly seek God's direction for the work, and for your own spiritual growth. Remember that you are, first and foremost, a human being. Among other things, that means you'll have stronger moments and weaker moments, and there will be times when the work God is doing is in you rather than through you. There will be times to tend to your own growth and well-being.

When those times come, don't be afraid to ask for help. Whether through the support of friends or the services of a professional counselor (or both), get the help you need to heal, to grow, and to move forward. Dolphus's and my experience has taught us that when you don't deal with issues—individual or relational—as they arise, things get worse, and gulfs get wider. Working through the problems, while it can certainly be painful, eventually brings about beautiful fruit in character, relationships and ministry.

I would add that it's important to be wise about the sources from which you seek help and advice. Well-meaning people can steer you in directions that aren't helpful if they don't really understand what you're going through. I would recommend looking for people who have experience in the kind of work you do, or the particular situation you're in, to help you cope with difficult problems or decisions. Again, it's not that people with different backgrounds or experience can't be of help—in fact, they're often able to offer a refreshing perspective when you're too close to something to see it clearly—but insight from others who have weathered similar storms is always of great value.

On a practical note, if you're going to work in rural or other community development ministry, you'll want to budget wisely and learn to be content with a modest lifestyle. There are likely to be some material things you would like to have but can't afford, and you'll be a lot happier if you've learned to be okay with that.

Finally, and this is a hard one to control, but it's vitally important: Love the people you serve. They'll know if you don't (and they'll know if you do), and it makes all the difference in the world. You may not be able to solve all, or even any, of their problems, but your love and concern for the people who turn to you for assistance are great gifts. Your affirmation of them as precious human beings and valuable members of the community will help them muster the strength and confidence they require to address the situations they face. Your willingness to listen to their stories will assure them that not only their needs, but their whole lives are important to you. Your love will fuel the hope that their futures can be "better" (more joy-filled, more productive, more stable—whatever "better" looks like for them) than their pasts.

And that's where I am today—able to look forward with hope because I can look backward and see how deeply God has loved me in the past. He's taken me on an amazing adventure filled with experiences and opportunities I never expected to have. I've ministered to others, and others have ministered to me. My journey has included great joy and great sorrow. There are some things I would change if I could, but since I can't, I simply pray that as I continue to walk with God, I'll gain a clearer understanding of who He's created me to be, and I'll find greater and greater fulfillment in serving Him well. When all is said and done, I pray that He will say, as Dolphus often does, "Whatever I asked Rosie to do, she did it, and people were blessed because she was willing to serve."